All the Things

endorsements

"There is so much wisdom packed into this small book. It is deep and reflective, yet practical and accessible for readers wanting to learn more about incorporating spiritual practices into their everyday life. Katie writes with excitement and passion out of a desire to share with others what has been so transformative for her. Reading *All The Things* feels like having a trusted friend walking with you and gently inviting you to pay attention to what God is doing in your life."

— **Jill Gullahorn**, Singer-Songwriter

"Sometimes we simply know. The first time I met Katie Haseltine, we were sitting together in the Art House in Nashville, and I listened, intrigued by her thoughtful passion for all things that should be. And now, over many years, my respect has only deepened as her life has deepened. She has worked hard to form her heart after the heart of God, and I have watched with affection and respect as she gives herself away to others, for others. I pray that this new book will bring her commitments and love to a wider world, a hope I have long had. *All the Things* is for everyone, everywhere, who longs for what should be, for what someday will be."

— **Steven Garber**, Author, *The Seamless Life: A Tapestry of Love and Learning, Worship and Work* Senior Fellow for Vocation and the Common Good for the M.J. Murdock Charitable Trust

"There may never have been a more critical time in our history than this for our world to receive a resource like *All the Things*. Our readiness to accept, understand, and practice the daily Examen is likely to make all the difference in our ability to exhibit self-leadership, find inner freedom, and respond to the urgent needs of our communities from a place of courage, compassion, and clarity. The Examen invites us to a crucial posture of pausing to pay attention, and from that place, new insights, motivations, and fresh energy arises. When we search our heart, mind, and body and can truly find God in all things, our experiences are re-framed—if not redeemed! Our world is desperate for people who are deeply rooted, grounded in themselves, their faith, and their values and are equally generous, considerate, and wholehearted. The Examen practice makes this possible."

— **Amy Alexander**, LMFT, Co-Founder and Executive Director, The Refuge Center for Counseling

"Reviving the ancient and practical Prayer of Examen, Katie accompanies readers on a 30-day journey into Christian spirituality and—ultimately—into experiences of God's love in one's real, concrete life and body. This is not a book simply to be read; it is an adventure to be lived and received by all who long for soul nourishment, presence, and Love."

— **Renee Farkas**, MA, Christian Spirituality Spiritual Director (specializing in Ignatian Spirituality) Founder of AmberNest Spiritual Direction, Franklin, Tennessee

"We've known Katie for more than two decades. In our twenties, we spent weekends together as married couples, eating and talking sun-up to sun-down. Which means that, in spite of all the life lived since then (the miles between us, the kids we've raised, the marital ups and downs we've experienced), we know Katie well. Our friendship was firmly established in those early days—along with her tendency to end every disagreement with 'Jesus.' For as long as we've known her, all Katie roads have led to Jesus. Any topic, any argument, any anything: Katie would remind us of a verse or idea that drew the conversation back to Him.

"And she's still doing it. *All the Things* is beautiful and authentic and interesting and profound and truth-filled and Jesus-focused… just like our friend."

— **Dallas and Amanda Jenkins**, Creators of *The Chosen*

"*All the Things* is a winsome invitation to grow your soul through a deeper exploration of Ignatian spirituality, contemplative living, and the Enneagram. Katie reintroduces readers to ancient pathways of spiritual practices with earthy, practical applications that we can all access in our modern lives. If you join Katie in the journey that she invites you to through *All the Things*, you may just find your heart, mind, and soul expanded—I certainly did! Don't miss the invitation!"

— **Hunter Mobley**, Enneagram Teacher
Author, *Forty Days on Being a Two*

"I have watched my wife embrace the rich, spiritual bounty of contemplative prayer for many years. It has meant the difference between a life tethered to anxiety and life characterized by peace. She hasn't simply written about a dusty ancient prayer practice; she has described the living, moving way God speaks to her and offers, generously, to guide the rest of us into that transformative sacred space."

— **Dan Haseltine**, Jars of Clay, Founder of Blood:Water

"In giving us a thorough description and practice of the Examen prayer, Katie has ushered her readers into an intimacy with God that I think we all desire and long for. Christianity in the United States has, from its origin, been heavily saturated with a mindset of 'doing' to achieve right standing with the Father. Katie graciously confronts that notion by introducing a simple, yet deeply profound practice that literally creates an intimate space with our Daddy where we can reflect, relate, and rest in His presence and His promises just by 'being.' I am grateful for the challenge of intimacy that I received as I read through her book and will be forever changed because of my practice of the Examen prayer. If a space can be created by which we relate deeply and intimately with God, it definitely is created as we posture our hearts, minds, and bodies properly to communicate with Him through the Examen prayer."

— **Anthony Hendricks**, Professor of Biblical Unity at Williamson College, Pastor, Co-Founder, The Public (an Anti-Racism organization in Franklin, Tennessee)

"Katie Haseltine does an amazing job guiding you from having knowledge of God to knowing Him intimately. In this journal, you will experience being held by Him and cherished on a deeper level and experience how God truly knows you, sees you, and loves you for exactly who you are… His beloved and cherished child. So, dive into this beautiful journal for a rich and transformative experience with God right beside you."

— **Beth McCord**, Your Enneagram Coach, Author, *Becoming Us: Using the Enneagram to Create a Thriving Gospel-Centered Marriage*

"If you've ever wondered where to find God in your mundane moments and groundhog days, *All the Things* is a good place to start. Katie Haseltine will teach you to pray in a forgiving, inviting, and flexible way. She doesn't offer easy answers, but her battle scars make her a trustworthy guide."

— **Steve Wiens**, Pastor of Genesis Covenant Church Author, *Shining Like the Sun*

"If new habits take 30 days to adopt, then *All the Things* may be a God-send. The Prayer of Examen is one of the most powerful tools I know to remember God's presence in every moment, and Katie Haseltine harnesses this remembering into 30 days of life-changing reflections."

—**Catherine McNiel**, Author of *Long Days of Small Things* and *All Shall Be Well*

all the things

A 30 DAY GUIDE TO EXPERIENCING GOD'S PRESENCE IN THE PRAYER OF EXAMEN

KATIE HASELTINE

NASHVILLE

NEW YORK • LONDON • MELBOURNE • VANCOUVER

All the Things

A 30 Day Guide to Experiencing God's Presence in the Prayer of Examen

© 2021 Katie Haseltine

All Scripture quotations, unless otherwise indicated, are taken from The Message. Copyright © 1993, 1994, 1995, 1996, 2000, 2001, 2002. Used by permission of NavPress Publishing Group.

Published in New York, New York, by Morgan James Publishing. Morgan James is a trademark of Morgan James, LLC. www.MorganJamesPublishing.com

Morgan James BOGO™

A **FREE** ebook edition is available for you or a friend with the purchase of this print book.

[ ]

CLEARLY SIGN YOUR NAME ABOVE

Instructions to claim your free ebook edition:
1. Visit MorganJamesBOGO.com
2. Sign your name CLEARLY in the space above
3. Complete the form and submit a photo of this entire page
4. You or your friend can download the ebook to your preferred device

ISBN 9781631954092 paperback
ISBN 9781631954108 ebook
Library of Congress Control Number: 2020950773

Cover Design by:
Dan Haseltine

Interior Design by:
Chris Treccani
www.3dogcreative.net

Author Photo by:
David Braud Photography
www.davidbraud.com

Morgan James PUBLISHING Builds

with...

Habitat for Humanity®
Peninsula and Greater Williamsburg

Morgan James is a proud partner of Habitat for Humanity Peninsula and Greater Williamsburg. Partners in building since 2006.

Get involved today! Visit
MorganJamesPublishing.com/giving-back

table of contents

The Prayer of Examen   *xiii*

Introduction   *xv*

Chapter 1	All the History about the Examen	3
Chapter 2	All the Gifts of the Examen	9
Chapter 3	All the Ways to Pray the Examen	13
Day 1:	Love	27
Day 2:	Ordinary	31
Day 3:	Movement	37
Day 4:	Waiting	47
Day 5:	Gratitude	53
Day 6:	Feelings	59
Day 7:	Ish	67
Day 8:	Curiosity	73
Day 9:	Savor	79
Day 10:	Self-Compassion	85
Day 11:	Boundaries	91
Day 12:	Forgiveness	97
Day 13:	Listen	103
Day 14:	Healing	109
Day 15:	Solitude	115
Day 16:	Notice	121
Day 17:	Simplicity	127
Day 18:	Rest	133

Day 19:   Generosity   139
Day 20:   Centers   145
Day 21:   Values   151
Day 22:   Location   157
Day 23:   Character   163
Day 24:   Serve   169
Day 25:   Now   175
Day 26:   Together   181
Day 27:   Inner Freedom   187
Day 28:   Practice   193
Day 29:   Desires   199
Day 30:   New   205
Conclusion   211

Acknowledgments   *213*
Appendix   *217*
Resources   *221*
About the Author   *225*

the prayer of examen

God, thank you.
I thank you, God, for always being with me, but especially I am grateful that you are with me right now.

God, send your Spirit upon me.
God, let the Holy Spirit enlighten my mind and warm my heart that I may know where and how we have been together this day.

God, let me look at my day.
God, where have I felt your presence, seen your face, heard your word this day? God, where have I ignored you, run from you, perhaps even rejected you this day?

God, let me be grateful and ask forgiveness.
God, I thank you for the times this day we have been together and worked together. God, I am sorry for the way that I have offended you by what I have done or what I did not do.

God, stay close.
God, I ask that you draw me ever closer to you this day and tomorrow. God, you are the God of my life—thank you.[1]

---

1   David L. Fleming, SJ, *What Is Ignatian Spirituality?* (Chicago, IL: Loyola Press, 2008), 21–22.

introduction

I truly believe that praying the Examen rescued me.

It was the summer of 2011, and my bruised and weary soul cried out for relief. With my husband away on tour (he's the lead singer for Jars of Clay) and my younger son dropped off in his Sunday school classroom, I stood on the hot pavement of the church parking lot and stared down my older, ten-year-old son. A reluctant churchgoer at best, he had opened the trunk of our mini-van and entrenched himself in the trunk.

He crossed his arms and refused to go to Sunday school.

I summoned my strength and resolved to win this battle if it was the last thing I did. Our combined stubbornness weighed heavier than the July humidity, and thirty minutes into our stand-off, in exasperation, I pleaded with him to tell me why he wouldn't go to Sunday school. His single sentence was the proverbial straw that broke the camel's back. He said, "I don't like how I feel when I'm in there."

His answer deflated my anger and frustration. It was then I suddenly realized with deep knowing that I felt the same way too. Something needed to change.

I made him go to church that day (I still had to win—every parent of a "spirited" child knows that all is lost if you give up everything) but let him choose where to sit. As I watched church unfold from the very back row of the sanctuary, I heard Jesus whisper gently to my heart, "You could take a break."

I was at a crossroads. I was exhausted from trying too hard—to be a good parent, to be a good Christian, to be a good ALL THE THINGS—and my soul needed something different. So, after fifteen years of membership, my husband and I left our home church to seek out something we weren't quite sure of. It was hard, messy, and painful, and I experienced the leaving as loss—even though I wanted and *needed* to go.

Thankfully, God did not leave us and instead, with great kindness, led us to a new church home where I could begin to name and understand the state of my soul.

I realized my head was full, but my heart was empty.

More than that, my head and heart were in an undesired battle for my soul. It was as if I were trying to walk down two different paths—one of *knowledge* of God and the other of *knowing* God—and God lifted me up above the opposing forces in my soul and set me down gently onto a wide, open path of harmony—a path where my head and my heart joined to know and love Jesus.

I took some time to think about how I got so tired, and my thoughts took me back to childhood.

When I was in grade school, my mom gave me an emerald green T-shirt with a sparkly, rainbow-colored iron-on that said, "Anything boys can do, girls can do better." I felt invincible in that shirt as I roamed the neighborhood with the other kids after school and on weekends.

My dad loved introducing me and my sister to his friends and colleagues (still does), and when he introduced me, it was always as the "first female President of the United States." My dream, even at that young age, was to go to college and become a lawyer, just like my dad. I believed—and was encouraged to believe—I could do anything.

So, I joined the cheer squad, ran for student council, shot bow and arrow, and, in college, served on the leadership team of Inter-Varsity Christian Fellowship.

But something wasn't quite right. After I came to faith in Jesus at seventeen, I started picking up on other messages—messages about what it means to be a "good Christian woman." Books, pastors, and friends all spoke about a Christian woman's need to focus on marriage and kids. I took this personally and desperately wanted to do the right thing.

I abandoned law school for a teaching degree because it was a more "family-friendly" career. I resigned my position in ICF because my pastor didn't believe in women in leadership. I was terribly confused. I didn't know anymore what I could do in the world.

The stark contrast of my childhood affirmation "You can do anything!" and my church teaching "You can do anything *except...*" created in me an enormous well of disillusionment and pain—which I tried to deny and ignore as I grew older and did the things I was supposed to do (get married, have kids, serve the church). All I knew to do was to keep trying to do the right thing as defined by the authorities in my life (I was nothing if not a compliant child).

My motto for years was, "Just tell me what to do and I'll do it."

I really believed that if I did ALL THE RIGHT THINGS, then everything would be okay. (The subtext of that belief is that "everything is up to me.") Piled on top of that self-imposed, impossible expectation was the assumption that if I knew all the right things *about* God, then I would *feel* close to God.

So many memories from my twenties and thirties contain the same elements: loneliness, trying hard, and weariness. My heart and soul wanted *so much more* and nothing I knew to do was working any longer. I was desperate for something beyond "doing," and my framework for understanding God and practicing my faith wasn't big enough to meet my need.

I think the best word to describe my relationship with God, the church, and Christianity at that time is "right." I focused on right theology, right thinking, right living. The condition of my heart was secondary to truth.

Of course, there is nothing wrong with truth or "right." But the combination of my personality plus my life's experiences plus how I interpreted the church's teachings was toxic and formed within me a tangled knot of half-truths and confused notions.

The problem was that I kept bumping up against the ache in my heart as I strove to live out all the right things about Jesus.

I could rattle off proof verses on "substitutionary atonement," but I did not feel comforted by my knowledge in my hurts and fears. I longed for actual Presence to meet me in my brokenness.

For the first time in my life, I didn't want to be right; I wanted to be *held*. I knew God loved me—even sang over me—but I wanted to feel it. To experience that love in the deepest parts of who I was. To believe that—as a woman—I was seen and known and loved. To know that there was meaningful work for me in this world too.

In my journal that fall, I wrote down what a trusted mentor shared with me, "Generosity is being willing to receive all that God has for me." I realized I was tired because I was hustling.

Hustling to do the right thing, fixing everything that was broken, knowing all the right things, serving in all the appropriate ways, and being the change that I wanted to see in the world. (Bless my earnest, well-intentioned heart.) The idea of receiving from God was alien to me, and yet it was the most inviting idea I'd heard in years. And the first gift God dropped into my outstretched hands was the Examen.

Encountering the Examen

After a summer of church visits, in the fall of 2011, my husband and I joined a Protestant liturgical church. I remember crying tears of relief and comfort as I listened to the chant-like songs week after week. The repetitive songs and prayers created some room for me to breathe—to sense an invitation to rest. The presence of women in leadership—in the front of the sanctuary even—made a way for me to enter into God's presence in a new way.

Not long after joining our new church, I met my first spiritual director. If spiritual direction or a spiritual director is new to you (like it was to me), let me introduce you. A spiritual director is simply a companion on your spiritual journey.

Spiritual direction is the process by which individuals learn to notice, listen to, and discern the movement or voice of God within their everyday experiences, thoughts, and feelings. The guide is the Holy Spirit and together the director and "directee" (the person receiving spiritual direction) pay attention to the Spirit's leading and prompting.

The role of the spiritual director is to provide a safe, loving environment for an individual to explore and sit with what God is offering. The goal of spiritual direction is not problem-solving or gaining knowledge but growing a relationship with God and self.

I don't remember much about my first meeting with Renee, the spiritual director from my new church, but I know I did most of the talking. Even though she asked maybe four questions and said very little, I walked away feeling lighter and hopeful.

We met again and she described the "Spiritual Exercises" to me. The Spiritual Exercises are a compilation of meditations, prayers, and contemplative practices developed by St. Ignatius to help people deepen their relationship with God.

She invited me to participate, along with four other women, in this at-home "Retreat in Daily Life."[2] I spent the next thirty-six weeks on an unforgettable journey into the life of Jesus. It was in the context of the Spiritual Exercises that I learned the Examen—an ancient prayer that is central to the Exercises.

As a part of doing the Spiritual Exercises, Renee instructed us to pray the Examen each day and journal our experience with it. Multiple versions of the Examen exist. This is the way I prayed it that year.

The Prayer of Examen

God, thank you for your presence.
I thank you for always being with me, but especially I am grateful that you are with me right now.

God, send your Spirit upon me.
Let the Spirit enlighten my mind and warm my heart that I may know where and how we have been together this day.

God, let me look at my day.
Where have I felt your presence, seen your face, heard your word this day? Show me what was good for me today—what warmed my heart and brought a smile to my face as I remembered it? Where was I? What was I doing? Who was I with?

Where have I ignored you, run from you, perhaps even rejected you this day? Show me the places in my day that lacked a felt sense of love and belonging. What do I regret or wish

---

2   There are several versions of the Spiritual Exercises—some are shorter and some longer. The one I did was called the 19th Annotation, or Retreat in Daily Life.

didn't happen? What desire arises when I remember? Do I want to ask God's forgiveness? Do I want to ask where God was in it? Do I want to change something in the future? Do I want to accept it and go on? I express my desires to God.

God, let me be grateful and ask forgiveness.
I thank you for all of the gifts of this day. I ask for healing and forgiveness for the times today when I wandered from your love.

God, stay close.
I ask that you draw me even closer to you this day and tomorrow. Help me recall a memory from the day or from another time in my life where I felt loved. Help me stay in that memory, held in love, savoring it as I fall asleep.

Praying Your Highs and Lows

When my kids were little, we would ask them at the dinner table, "What were your highs and lows from today?" I'd read somewhere that asking kids, "Did you have a good day?" could create unwanted pressure to respond in a certain way. The question assumes that their day should be good and, if it wasn't, there is no room to discuss the hard. Also, it's a yes or no question—"yeah" or "nah" might be all you get (I have sons, so this IS the realm of my possibility.).

We were trying to get them to notice a specific moment or event and describe it for us in order to get to know them. We wanted to provide our own answers in order for them to get to know us. High/low also presupposes that there are ups and downs in every normal day and every kind of story is welcome at the table. (As Fred Rogers is famous for saying, "What is mentionable is manageable.")

The Examen assumes a similar idea: There is something both high and low to notice about your day. Examen (or Examen of Consciousness as some call it) is a prayer that provides structure for you to reflect on your day and pick out the highs and lows. Every kind of story is welcome in your recounting—God is able and willing to hold them all. In telling God the ups and downs, you get to know each other. The added gift of the Examen is that, as you explore your day, it draws you to the awareness of God's presence, generosity, forgiveness, and support.

Taking a Look at the Examen

At a glance, the Examen is:

1. **God, thank you for your presence:** An opportunity to remind yourself of the presence of God.
2. **God, send your Spirit upon me:** A moment to ask for help from the Spirit.
3. **God, let me look at my day:** A way to organize and see the events of your day.
4. **God, let me be grateful and ask for forgiveness:** A time to offer thanks and request forgiveness for how you've forgotten who you are and Whose you are.
5. **God, stay close:** A point of connection and grounding in the request for God to be close to you tomorrow.

The Examen is also:

- **A daily prayer:** Any time, day or night, works as you simply review your day from the time you made your last Examen to the present moment (try to stick to a twenty-four-hour time period to not get overwhelmed). The prayer "works" because you need only a day's worth of thoughts, feelings, and interactions to begin. You can show up as you are, feeling as you do any day you choose.

- **A short prayer:** The practice typically lasts ten minutes. You may find it leads to a longer, deeper encounter with God—or you may notice that even a three-minute review offers insight and hope.
- **An honest prayer:** Honesty matters. In reflecting on your responses throughout the day, you tell the truth about yourself and God and draw grace into your awareness. Truth, in this context, doesn't hurt but ushers in healing and connection with yourself and God. God already knows all the things. So do you. When you talk it over together, you increase your intimacy and trust with God.
- **A light prayer:** Examen is not meant to be a long, heavy exercise. It is to be a light, open glance at the day that allows its fragments to be recollected in God.
- **A recollection prayer:** All the things will run through your mind as you pray. Keep a journal to help you remember them all. Journal anything that seems noteworthy. I recommend writing down your insights as it provides a way to look back and notice patterns and common themes.

PART 1

—

get to know the examen

chapter 1

ALL THE HISTORY
ABOUT THE EXAMEN

—

The Examen exposed me to a different, contemplative stream of Christianity that I never knew existed. It got me curious about St. Ignatius—the man who popularized this ancient prayer practice—and all the things that make up Ignatian Spirituality. If history is not your thing, feel free to skip to the next chapter to read about the gifts of praying the Examen.

The Story of St. Ignatius of Loyola

Let's start with Ignatius. If you are like me, you wouldn't plan a month-long trip with someone you haven't met. You also wouldn't trust the words of someone unless you knew their story, knew where they were coming from. So, I want you to meet St. Ignatius, this unlikely friend of mine, and join us on this journey into the Examen.

He is not without fault, and I am not without error in my interpretation of who he is. But what we share in common—a love of Jesus—places us on the same road more often than not. (Hang in there with me through the next bit—it's difficult to spice up the life of a saint.)

Born into nobility in 1491 in Loyola, Spain, Ignatius spent his youth traveling, studying art and literature, and training for war. After serving the Spanish King at court and in the army, in 1517, Ignatius joined the Spanish army. In 1521, during a battle with the French, a cannonball shattered his lower left leg. Badly injured, Ignatius was taken to his family castle in Loyola where he endured two painful surgeries and months of recovery.

While he recuperated, Ignatius asked for romance novels to read. Tales of love and war were the favorite fodder for his imagination and daydreams, but the only books available to him were those about the life of Christ and stories about saints. He was given *The Life of Jesus Christ* by Ludolph of Saxony, *The Golden Legend*, a collection of the lives of the saints by Jacobus de Voragine, and *Imitation of Christ* by Thomas à Kempis.

An observant man by nature, he began to notice how he felt after reading religious books compared to how he experienced romance novels. He discovered that the stories of Jesus and the saints inspired and stimulated him, while stories of love and war unsettled and disappointed him. He noticed that he went to sleep feeling peaceful and full of joy after he imagined himself as one of the saints who gave his life away to God.

David Fleming, SJ,[3] a Jesuit author and teacher, describes the internal movements of Ignatius's soul during his recovery like this:

> Gradually, a new and inspiring image of God began to form in Ignatius's mind. He saw God as a God of Love.

---

3   SJ indicates a member of the Society of Jesus, or a Jesuit. The Society of Jesus is a Roman Catholic order founded by St. Ignatius.

This was no abstract philosophical concept. God as Love was no longer just a scriptural statement. Ignatius experienced God as an intensely personal, active, generous God, a God as Love loving. God creates, and by so doing God is actively showering us with gifts....Lying on his sickbed—in pain, crippled, agitated—Ignatius came to understand that active loving was God's most outstanding quality. This is his foundational image of God. He arrived at it by "noting" how God dealt with him in his body, soul, and spirit, and through the people and events in his everyday life.[4]

The Spiritual Exercises

With a new understanding of God's love and healing from his injury, Ignatius went on a pilgrimage in 1522 to a monastery near Montserrat. He spent time there, and then in a cave, examining his life and heart. He suffered months of doubts and temptations, followed by deep and refreshing encounters with God.

He composed much of what we now refer to as *The Spiritual Exercises* during his time of solitude in the cave and continued to add to them over the next eleven years as he traveled all over Europe as a student, preacher, and teacher.

The Spiritual Exercises were published in 1548. They have since been translated into hundreds of languages and used by people from every walk of life. For centuries, the Exercises were given over a thirty-day retreat in solitude to prospective Jesuits. In fact, every Jesuit priest makes this retreat at least twice during his training for the priesthood, and it serves as the basis of his annual retreat too.

In recent years, a movement to make the Exercises available to everyone led to the development of a thirty-six-week "retreat"

---

4   Fleming, *What Is Ignatian Spirituality?*, 8–9.

that could be done in-between working, making dinner, caring for loved ones, and mowing the lawn. There are several annotations (or versions) of the Exercises to choose from now. Traditionally, you "make" the Spiritual Exercises with a spiritual director—either individually or in a group.

The Society of Jesus

Ignatius chose to spread his message of a loving, active God among the poor and outcast and faced persecution in the form of imprisonment, beatings, and expulsions from cities for his message and methods. By 1534, he had gathered nine others to join his ministry. Together they took vows of poverty, chastity, and obedience to God and the Pope and several years later officially formed the Society of Jesus, or Jesuits.

When Ignatius died in 1556, there were over 1,000 Jesuits. There are over 16,000 today. The most famous Jesuit is Jorge Mario Bergoglio who became Pope Francis, the 266th pope of the Roman Catholic Church, in 2013. Pope Francis is the first Jesuit to be elected Pope.

Ignatian Spirituality

"Ignatian Spirituality" (the term used to describe the teachings of St. Ignatius) is simply an approach to Christian spirituality based on insights Ignatius gained throughout his life and written about in *The Spiritual Exercises*.

While St. Ignatius is deeply rooted in the Catholic tradition, his insights are valuable to anyone of any religious background who seeks to know God better. The roots of Ignatian Spirituality lie in the Scriptures and in an understanding of the person of Jesus. Ignatius, then, is just another guide on the journey home to God.

A pastor friend often says that the particular denomination he aligns with is not the only way to practice Christian faith, but a faithful way. I've found Ignatian Spirituality to be a faithful way to live out my Christianity as I've navigated the ups and downs of living in this world full of goodness and evil. It's helped me be honest about the darkness (in myself, others, and the world) while holding onto the light.

The First Principle and Foundation

The Principle and Foundation, a reflection at the beginning of the Spiritual Exercises, provides a quick overview of Ignatian spirituality:

The goal of our life is to live with God forever. God, who loves us, gave us life. Our own response of love allows God's life to flow into us without limit.

All the things in this world are gifts of God, presented to us so that we can know God more easily and make a return of love more readily.

As a result, we appreciate and use all these gifts of God insofar as they help us develop as loving persons. But if any of these gifts become the center of our lives, they displace God and so hinder our growth toward our goal.

In everyday life, then, we must hold ourselves in balance before all of these created gifts insofar as we have a choice and are not bound by some obligation. We should not fix our desires on health or sickness, wealth or poverty, success or failure, a long life or short one. For everything has the potential of calling forth in us a deeper response to our life in God.

Our only desire and our one choice should be this: I want and I choose what better leads to God's deepening his life in me.[5]

This is what I get out of the First Principle and Foundation:

- God loves me. I love because God first loved me.
- It's not supposed to be hard to find God in the world—and my life.
- God wants to be known.
- God provides ways to help us love better.
- Everything and anything can help me know and love God.

Finding God in All Things

A popular Jesuit catch phrase is "finding God in all things." My hope is to show you how to use the Examen prayer to find God—particularly God's presence—in all the things of your life.

5   Fleming, *What Is Ignatian Spirituality?*, 2–3.

chapter 2

ALL THE GIFTS OF THE EXAMEN

—

The Move from Being Right to Being Loved

In the spring of 2020, I was enjoying a much-needed solo day retreat in a friend's carriage house. After two months cooped up in my house with my family, I needed some space to think and to reconnect with myself and God.

I brought with me that day a book I wanted to read, some prayers I needed to pray, and—a last minute addition—the journals from praying the Examen during the Spiritual Exercises nine years ago. I had a sense that God wanted to remind me of all I had learned during that time.

God used the Examen to gently guide me from a place where I knew about God into a wide-open space where I knew God. I found in the prayer a faithful path to greater faith, hope, and love in Jesus. Praying the Examen offered me an opportunity to encounter the heart of Jesus and shift my focus from being right to being loved.

After immersing myself in being loved, I lost almost all my taste for being right in everyone else's eyes (at least about theology anyway—when it comes to my kids I still want them to think I'm right about ALL the things). I needed to be loved by Jesus—and I wanted to offer my love in return—on that chilly spring day. The best thing I knew to do was to go back to the prayer that changed everything for me.

Seeds Are Still Growing

Three hours after picking up the first journal, I sat back with tears in my eyes, grateful all over again for my year with a sixteenth century warrior turned priest named St. Ignatius of Loyola. I knew at the time that the Examen (and the Spiritual Exercises) changed me. I didn't realize how much until I reread all that I had written. I was struck most of all by the recognition that what I learned was still enlarging my heart—still breathing life into my soul.

Here are a few things I noticed from my journals:

- Psalm 23:6 is a significant verse for me. "Your beauty and love chase after me every day of my life." (MSG) "Surely goodness and mercy shall follow me all the days of my life." (ESV) In my early twenties, the song "Love's Been Following You" by Twila Paris was the soundtrack in my head. During times of transition and suffering, this verse pops up over and over—and I found it all throughout my time in the Exercises and in what I noticed when I prayed the Examen.

- At the start of the Exercises, we were asked to collect items from outside to represent our feelings or ideas about God. In my journal, I wrote regarding that assignment, "Nature doesn't do a lot for me." I was aghast to see that sentence. It seemed so out of sync with who I am today. I'm obsessed with the ocean (any body of water really), the mountains, walks outside. I think what I meant then is that I didn't connect creation with its Creator. I didn't see or experience God in nature. What a difference from how I connect to God today. The lesson for me here is that people do change—and they do wake up to what they don't see at first. Thanks be to God.

- I returned to Isaiah 58:11 often. "The Lord will always lead you, satisfy you in a parched land…" (CSB) The weight of the world felt heavy to me then, and I wrote about looking in the mirror, expecting to see a much older woman, and feeling surprised when a thirty-something one stared back at me. I remember the burden that idea placed on me and how forefront it was in my mind. I no longer connect to that image of an older woman. I've experienced so much healing and continue to see how God heals me.

- The humility and love of Jesus oozed off the pages. Over and over I wrote about how Jesus had burrowed his way under my skin and found the way to my heart. I read the stories of Jesus in the temple at age twelve and Jesus healing the woman who touched his hem and discovered the love that I had been longing to find.

The Examen Is Worth Sharing

When I reread my journal observations, it was so obvious that the Examen was the common thread that ran through every page. Ignatius is often quoted as saying that if Jesuits can pray only one prayer a day, it should be the Examen.

The purpose of the prayer, which was evident in my journals, is to notice God's presence in the daily events of life. My journals affirmed that everything I was able to see—the importance of Psalm 23, God in nature, the healing of my sorrows, and the love of Jesus—was possible because I practiced the Examen.

Being reminded of the importance of the Examen delighted my spiritual director's heart. There is no prayer practice I offer more than the Examen. I see its impact on people's souls on a regular basis. And now I had my own journals with proof of its gifts to me over the last nine years.

As I sat there taking in the full measure of God's grace to me, the whisper of a book idea slowly formed in my mind. I brushed it off initially (having never written a book before) but the whisper grew louder and louder until I knew that I would write a 30-day guide to praying the Examen—for you.

A reality that compelled me, despite my fears about writing a book on the Examen, is that I was twenty years into my spiritual journey before I stumbled upon this gentle path. And when I sought out books to learn more, I found books mostly written by single, male priests—loving, empathic, knowledgeable male Jesuits to be sure—but very little written by someone like me.

The Examen is the most accessible prayer form I've used in thirty years of praying. Its insistence that all things speak of God's presence and activity in our lives makes it attainable to every type of person, from a celibate priest to a mother of sons. My desire to give this prayer greater exposure and attention gradually overwhelmed any doubts in my abilities as a writer.

While I've journaled my way through young adulthood into middle age, I never thought of myself as a writer. What I am is a *reader*. Books shape, challenge, and teach me. No significant change to my emotional and spiritual life occurs without the influence of books. So, I take what I've embarked on—writing a book—seriously. And I care that what I write makes sense to you and helps you.

chapter 3

ALL THE WAYS TO PRAY
THE EXAMEN

—

Pray the Examen as Yourself

So, thank you for picking this up and letting your curiosity or sorrow or doubt or sense of adventure guide you to these words. I'm glad you're here. I wish more than anything that we were in my sunroom—eye to eye, heart to heart—as we talk about all the things. But I'm grateful for books that make us friends, give us companionship when time, distance, schedules, and energy levels prevent it.

I offer you the Examen as a gift. My hope is that you find God when you pray the Examen. I wish I could GIVE you everything you need to, once and for all, know God's love for you, unlock the healing you've been longing for, and become more like Jesus.

All I've got is this ancient practice that, over the years, has changed how I think about so many things. So, do with this book what you want. You may choose to "read" it all in one sitting for the information. Some of you will "pray" one entry per day like a devotional. I wouldn't be surprised if some of you start it, forget about it, and pick it back up three years from now after a conversation with a friend causes you to remember it.

What I know is that you will get what you need from it, when you need it—that's one of the truths this practice has shown me.

I also want you to be yourself as you engage the Examen. Born in rural Pennsylvania, I am in my mid-forties and, as of two years ago, have spent more than half of my life in the suburbs of Tennessee. I have divorced parents (who are still friends), one biological younger sister, one adopted younger sister, and three stepsiblings. I'm an Enneagram One and the mother of boys.

My point is that I write this book with a unique lens and yours will not be the same. The gift of the Examen is that it doesn't ask you to conform to one idea of a devout practitioner. If you bring yourself, your story, and your last twenty-four hours, then you will have all you need. The practice is expansive enough to accommodate every kind of personality type.

Pray the Examen with Help from Enneagram Knowledge

One of the tools I use in my spiritual direction practice is the Enneagram. (I found myself using it so much that I decided to become a certified Enneagram coach several years later.) Before I learned to notice God in praying the Examen, the Enneagram taught me to pay attention to myself and notice my own patterns of behavior.

If this is the first time you've read the word Enneagram (pronounced eh nee uh gram), let me run quickly through a few things.[6] The Enneagram is based on the idea that there are nine

---

6 This is not a book about the Enneagram, nor will it explore in detail how each type encounters the Examen or God. But just as the Exercises and the Examen permeate my thinking, so does Enneagram wisdom. It may be helpful to tell you a little bit about it so you will have the full picture of where I'm coming from.

basic ways of seeing or engaging the world. The nine basic ways, or personalities, are labeled One through Nine. Enneagram wisdom teaches that you are born one type and stay the same throughout your life.

As Beth McCord, an Enneagram teacher, shares in her book *Becoming Us: Using the Enneagram to Create a Thriving Gospel-Centered Marriage*, one way to think about the Enneagram is like an internal GPS that shows you where you are (in your patterns of thinking, feeling, and doing) and where you are going (what growth might look like for you). Unlike Myers-Briggs and several other typing systems, the Enneagram is dynamic, not static, and offers you a way to grow toward the fullest expression of who God made you to be (your true self).

Enneagram wisdom further teaches that four core motivations are driving your personality: a fear, a desire, a weakness, and a longing.[7] We are all running toward something. The Enneagram calls this our Core Desire. Each of us believes that if we achieve this desire (internal peace, knowledge, safety, etc.), all of life will be okay. The less healthy we are, the more we will do to be okay. Your personality is defined by which core desire you run toward.

Along with running toward something, we are all running away from something. The Enneagram calls this our Core Fear. Each of us believes it is vital to our well-being to spend time and energy avoiding what we fear (incompetence, pain, conflict, etc.). The less healthy we are, the more we will do to avoid it.

Your Core Weakness (pride, gluttony, sloth, etc.) is the struggle you will wrestle with your whole life. The main point here is that the Core Weakness is like your Achilles heel—or the thorn in

---

7   Beth McCord and Jeff McCord, *Becoming Us: Using the Enneagram to Create a Thriving Gospel-Centered Marriage* (Nashville: Morgan James Publishing, 2020).

your flesh. Your Core Longing is what you have sought in every one of your key relationships—and what others have fallen short of giving you in those relationships.

This is what it looks like for me as an Enneagram One. My Core Desire is to be good or right, and my Core Fear is to be bad or wrong. I spend a lot of time figuring out what the rules are and what people expect of me. My Core Weakness is resentment—a simmering anger that leads to continual frustration and dissatisfaction with myself, others, and the world for not being perfect. My Core Longing is to be told, "You are good." I want the people I love to see how hard I'm trying to be the best I can be. If this sounds exhausting to you, you are correct. And your bag of tricks is just as tiring to you.

The gift of the Enneagram is that it shows me the way out of my particular rut in thinking, feeling, and doing. It also gives me deep compassion for myself (and others) as I see clearly how difficult it is to go against these unconscious patterns. Nothing, in fact, has given me greater self-compassion than the Enneagram. It allows me to see myself with grace—with God's kind eyes. When you experience yourself as God created you to be—without running from your fear or doing whatever is necessary to achieve your desire—you begin to reflect the characteristics of God as only you can with the personality you've been given.

What matters for you is the awareness that you are uniquely you and that you bring a specific lens to any spiritual practice—in this case, the Examen. For this book, I invited many of my directees, fellow spiritual directors, and friends to share their own stories about the Examen so you could see for yourself the variety of ways God uses this prayer in the lives of all kinds of people.

Pray the Examen with Your Heart, Mind, and Body

As I've worked with people over the years, I've noticed a few things that seem to make a difference when you pray the Examen—the posture of your heart, the posture of your mind, and the posture of your body. You are created to use all three in your communication with God.[8]

Heart Posture
- Open | Listen for what might rise from the day.
- Aware | Intentionally become aware of who you are in God and your deepest desire of knowing God and experiencing God's nearness and presence in your day.
- Trusting | Trust that whatever comes up is worthy of reflection.

Mind Posture
- Quieted | Take a few deep breaths. Rest a few minutes in God's love and presence.
- Non-Judgmental Observer | You might imagine yourself sitting with Jesus next to a stream and watching the events of the day float by. As a memory of the day comes to mind, reflect on it, and notice how aware you were of God's presence. Resist the urge to analyze, fix, or dig for more memories. Prayerfully allow more fragments of the day to arise. Continue to notice your awareness of God. If you did see God, express gratitude. If you did not see God, you might express your desire to see God in all things. In doing so, you are noticing both the hidden presence of God in the

---

8   More about this in "Day 20: Centers." Enneagram wisdom has a lot to offer here as well.

events of the day as well as your way of participating in, resisting, or missing that presence.

- Receptive | Receive what comes to mind, resisting the urge to judge it or dismiss it.

Body Posture

(Each individual has to figure out for themselves what works for their own body. I've provided a list of options. Play with it and see which posture is most helpful to you.)

- Still—if that is what you need to be present. Work with how God made you.
- Moving—if that is what you need to be present. Work with how God made you.
- On your knees—if humility is needed or wanted.
- Palms up—if your intent is to receive.
- Palms down—if your intent is to surrender.
- Hands up—if you long to praise.
- Eyes closed—if it helps you focus.
- Eyes open—if it helps you focus.

Pray the Examen in a Place

> *"Go into your room, close the door and pray to your Father,*
> *who is unseen."*
> — Jesus (Matthew 6:6 [NIV])

Sometime in the third century, men and women began to flee the cities of the Roman Empire in search of deeper spiritual truth. The desert fathers and mothers, as they were called, were ordinary Christians living in solitude in the deserts of Egypt, Palestine, Syria, and Arabia who chose to renounce the world in order to deliberately and individually follow God's call.

They embraced lives of celibacy, labor, fasting, prayer, and poverty, believing that denouncing material goods and practicing self-discipline would lead to unity with God. Their spiritual practice formed the basis of Western monasticism and greatly influenced both Western and Eastern Christianity.

Place mattered to these men and women who believed that to be holy meant to be set apart from society. They chose to express their belief in extreme ways by leaving their homes and living alone in huts and in caves.

Monasteries and convents exist today in continuation of their ideals. Very few of us do or ever will live in huts, caves, monasteries, or convents. But I wonder if we can take a piece of the wisdom they lived and use it for our own spiritual growth.

Abba Moses said in the early fourth century, "Sit in thy cell and thy cell will teach thee all." (Cell isn't exactly a happy word for us in modern day America. In 400 AD, cell called to mind solitude, smallness, and simplicity.) By the later fourth and fifth centuries, nuns and monks took this wisdom to heart and were encouraged to pick a monastery or community and remain there for the duration of their religious life.

One desert mother in particular, Amma Syncletica, used the metaphor of a nest to encourage others to stay put. She taught, "Just as the bird who abandons the eggs she was sitting on prevents them from hatching, so the monk or nun grows cold and their faith dies when they go from one place to another."

While her counsel refers to physical location, the deeper meaning involves not running from yourself. Amma Syncletica has a lot to offer those of us who move from one place to another, one distraction to another, or one voice to another. Spiritual growth and presence take time and patience—things in which we are not naturally gifted. "The wisdom the desert mothers offer us is that by staying with ourselves, with our inner ups and downs, with our hurts and our fears, we will bring forth the new life that God is creating within us. The [nest] teaches us to trust in the Presence even when it feels like absolutely nothing is happening."[9]

Creating a "nest" where we can lay on the "eggs" of what we are learning teaches us that transformation in love happens over a long period of time, and many days, it feels as if nothing is really happening.

When I started praying the Examen, I recognized that I didn't have a "nest" that was my own for reading, praying, and journaling. At the time, we lived in a smaller ranch house with no office or study. I scoured Craigslist and found a small, yellow wingback chair with a tear on the right arm for $50. I promise you there was no room for a chair in that 10x14 bedroom that already was full to bursting with a king-sized bed, end tables, and dressers. I moved things around and shoved the chair in the corner beside the window. I filled a basket with everything I would need (pens, journals, Bible, tissue) and hung a meaningful photo on the wall above the chair.

I won't soon forget the countless hours I spent in that chair. I fell in love with Jesus in a new way, rubbing my right thumb back and forth over that tear. On days when I had no energy, will, or feeling to sit and pray the Examen, I plopped down on that chair and simply acknowledged the presence of God in that place. Or I didn't. But 90 percent of the time I got up from that chair and felt better for having returned to a place of safety and learning.

---

9   Mary C. Earle, *The Desert Mothers: Spiritual Practices from the Women of the Wilderness* (London: Continuum, 2007), 23.

As you begin praying the Examen, identify a "nest" in your home to return to, day after day, week after week. While there is nothing magical about sitting in the same spot, the practice invites you to stillness and remembrance every time you come to it.

One of my directees chose a specific seat at her kitchen table. She liked the way the light came in through the windows in the early morning. Another directee took a nightly bath and chose to pray the Examen each evening in the tub. The location is not as important as the practice of sitting still in the same place over time.

Sitting in the same spot each day or evening also offers you a place to collapse when you have nothing to give. The spot reminds you that this is about what God offers you, not what you offer God. Vow to speak to yourself with love and compassion in that spot and you will begin hearing the loving whispers of the Divine whenever you sit there. There should be one place in the world where you belong, where you are loved, where you know your worth.

- Pick your spot. A chair, the bed, the porch, a stair. Some place for you to claim as your "nest" with God. Find your own "chair with a tear."

- Go outdoors if that is where you sense God's presence in the deepest way. John Muir said, "Everybody needs beauty as well as bread, places to play in and pray in, where nature may heal and give strength to body and soul."

- Gather objects, books, and pictures that matter to you and place them near your spot. Your gathered items themselves can also be your spot—wherever you sit with your basket of treasured belongings becomes your nest for that day.

- Sit each day. God is present to you there.

Pray the Examen with Love

A passage of Scripture that informs my practice of praying the Examen is in the book of Matthew. A religious expert asks Jesus to tell him the greatest commandment. Jesus replies, "'Love the Lord your God with all your heart and with all your soul and with all your mind.' This is the first and greatest commandment. And the second is like it: 'Love your neighbor as yourself.' All the Law and the Prophets hang on these two commandments." (Matthew 22:36–40 [NIV])

Stunning. Jesus sums up everything God said to humans with these two commandments to love. And the two commandments link the love of God to the love of others to the love of self. Many interpretations exist of these verses. The one that resonates with what I know about Jesus is this—our ability to receive the love of God allows us to return love to God and give it to others.

The way we know if we've received the love of God is by observing the way we talk to, care for and treat ourselves. Maya Angelou says it best, "I don't trust people who don't love themselves and tell me, 'I love you.' … There is an African saying which is: Be careful when a naked person offers you a shirt."

Love of God and love of self are more interconnected than I once thought. I believed that personal piety (doing right) was the point of Christian faith. I became convinced through the Examen, however, that it is more about the awareness of and the ability to receive God's love. And I can know if love is getting in by observing the way I interact with myself, my kids, my friends—and the driver going too slow in front of me on any ordinary day.

The method I use to pay attention to my interactions is the Examen. The Examen invites me to become an observer of my own life and heart—my feelings, thoughts, and actions. My prayers go with you as you "examine" your own life with this simple prayer.

Now... Pray!

That's it. That's the whole idea of the Examen. Seems simple, right? It is!

And placing yourself in front of God and offering up your days are profoundly life-changing. In the second half of the book, I hope to show you the many variations of Examen and the endless ways to pray it. I want to share with you specific ways I've grown from the Examen. I also want you to read the stories of my friends and directees and hear what the Examen means to them.

At the end of every day, in the "All the MORE" section, you will find questions for reflection, prayers, and practices to continue your Examen journey. Stay with what bears fruit. Lean into what draws you closer to faith, hope, and love. Take what you like and leave the rest.

The most important thing to know about the Examen is that you can't mess it up.

There isn't a wrong way to pray it.

If you fall asleep praying it each night, you end your day with your heart and mind turned toward God. If you try it in the mornings and get interrupted by your dog or your own distracted thoughts, you started your day with the intention of finding God.

The Examen is the most forgiving, inviting, flexible prayer you can pray.

May God be with you as you go!

PART 2

—

pray the examen for 30 days

day 1: love

"And now these three remain: faith, hope and love.
But the greatest of these is love."
— 1 Corinthians 13:13 (NIV)

If you practice the Examen, you will get a lot out of it. I know you will. But none of that matters—you will have nothing or gain nothing—if love isn't the foremost grace you receive and the main response you give back when you pray it.

The whole point is intimacy with God—an intimate relationship in which you share everything with Jesus, and he shares everything with you. There is nothing Jesus withheld from you—not his body, heart, life, or death. The work of a lifetime is to respond to that kind of love with openheartedness and generosity.

I asked someone once, "Do you know that God loves you?" My question was met with a dazed and confused stare. I went on, "You know, a feeling that you are known, a sense that you aren't alone, some awareness that you are delighted in or enjoyed. Beyond what you've read or been told, do you know, deep in your heart and soul, that the one who made you loves you?" The blank look I received told me the whole story. I don't know why some people know this love and why some struggle to feel it—I just know that some of you who picked up this book wish you knew more love than you do right now.

So, that is my hope for you. That somewhere in these pages, that somewhere on a chair in your home or on a bank beside a river, your soul would flood with warmth, your eyes would fill with tears, and your chest would burn with knowing—all because of the extravagant, relentless, gentle, generous love of God. I know some of you would rather not. You're not the kind of person who "burns" or "gets warm" with feeling. I get it. And I'm still going to pray it happens to you. I can't think of a better prayer for you as you begin your journey with the Examen than these verses out of Ephesians 3:16–19:

> And I ask him that with both feet planted firmly on love, you'll be able to take in with all followers of Jesus the extravagant dimensions of Christ's love. Reach out and experience the breadth! Test its length! Plumb the depths! Rise to the heights! Live full lives, full in the fullness of God.

And as I'm praying Ephesians over you, I hope the Suscipe prayer (St. Ignatius included this prayer at the end of *The Spiritual Exercises*) becomes your prayer to God:

> Take, Lord, and receive all my liberty, my memory, my understanding, and my entire will—all I have and call my own. You have given all to me. To you, Lord, I return it. Everything is yours; do with it what you will. Give me only your love and your grace, that is enough for me.

Part of what I love so much about a liturgical church is all the prayers you can borrow—prayers that have been prayed for hundreds of years. But if even these borrowed prayers feel like too much effort or are not authentic to your experience, keep looking for what fits. Maybe this prayer from Thomas Merton's *Thoughts in Solitude* is more how you are feeling as you begin.

> My Lord God, I have no idea where I am going. I do not see the road ahead of me. I cannot know for certain where it will end. Nor do I really know myself, and the fact that I think I am following your will does not mean that I am actually doing so. But I believe that the desire to please you does in fact please you. And I hope I have that desire in all that I am doing.

If that's still too much, if you are skeptical or wounded or bruised or tired, then come to the Examen like you would pull up a chair to the fire pit in your backyard. Not the kind where you have to chop wood, gather kindling, light it, and stoke it. But the gas kind where you get to flip a switch and the flames magically appear. That kind of fire.

Come to the Examen like you would pull up a chair to a fire.

As Desmond Tutu said, "Like when you sit in front of a fire in winter—you are just there in front of the fire. You don't have to be smart or anything. The fire warms you." So, let it. Let the fire do what it's meant to do. Just sit there in front of it until you thaw out—until you can feel your fingers again—until you can feel again. Let the sitting be your own version of a prayer.

ALL THE MORE

- As you pray the Examen today, ask that God would show you the deep and wide love that is for all God has made—especially you.
- Think about this remarkable quote in Corrie Ten Boon's *The Hiding Place*, "Do you know what hurts so very much? It's love. Love is the strongest force in the world, and when it is blocked that means pain. There are two things we can do when this happens. We can kill that love so that it stops hurting. But then, of course, part of us dies too. Or we can ask God to open up another route for that love to travel." If you struggle to feel God's love for you, confess that to God. Ask for help. Ask for help to see what blocks you. And then ask for a new path on which God's love can travel to your heart.
- Is there anything keeping you from pulling your chair up to the fire? Tell God about it. And be gentle with yourself as you come. You may have been burned by the fire. It's okay to feel a little scared.

day 2: ordinary

"God works in all things that exist; therefore, our intimate thoughts, feelings, desires, fears, and our responses to the people and things around us are not just the accidental ebb and flow of our inner lives, but rather the privileged moments through which God creates and sustains a unique relationship with each of us."
— *A Pocket Guide to Jesuit Education*

One of my favorite aspects of the Examen is how everyone is qualified and prepared to pray it simply because you've had a day. It may have been a good day or a bad day, but either way, you've lived the last twenty-four hours, and that means you've got something to pray about.

Most of us won't have a life-altering experience today. We will prepare and eat meals, exercise our bodies (hopefully), make the bed, talk to a friend, answer emails, watch or read the news, run an errand, and walk the dog. Dennis Hamm, SJ, says it this way, "If we are to listen for the God who creates and sustains us, we need to take seriously and prayerfully the meeting between the creatures we are and all else that God holds lovingly in existence. That 'interface' is the felt experience of my day."[10] The ordinary events of an everyday life add up to something when they are brought before God in the Examen.

A spiritual director friend of mine, Nancy, has been practicing the Examen for twenty years as the last prayer of her day. Her spiritual director taught it to her using the story of Jesus feeding the 5,000. In Nancy's words: "She invited me to wonder, 'Why do you think the apostles were asked to pick up the fragments that were left over?' She offered the idea that they picked up the fragments so they could fathom what God had just done. I hung onto the alliteration of "fragments and fathom." As I kneel beside my bed each night, I picture myself with a basket under my arm going chronologically through my day picking up the fragments of my day. If there is a difficult experience, I hold it a while and invite God to show me more. If it is an easy experience with joy and blessing, I praise God for it."

Fragments and fathom. Two words that encourage us to view the ordinary as sacred. A fragment of something implies that it is part of a whole. I don't know about you, but I've rarely been given a whole picture of anything from God. I'm shown the pieces of the puzzle over time, and only when I look back can I see how everything

Fragments and fathom.

was working toward one end or goal. And only when I see what God has been up to the whole time can I fathom the goodness and grace in it. Picking up the fragments in the Examen sets me up to

---

10   Dennis Hamm, SJ, "Rummaging for God: Praying Backwards through Your Day," Ignatian Spirituality, October 9, 2020, https://www.ignatianspirituality.com/ignatian-prayer/the-examen/rummaging-for-god-praying-backward-through-your-day/.

offer gratitude and thanksgiving as pieces fall into place—in big and small circumstances in my life.

Recently, I watched through the kitchen window as my son climbed into a friend's car. Just the night before we had discussed with him the importance of limiting the number of passengers in the car when you are a new driver. I pretended not to see that the number of kids exceeded what we had agreed was reasonable and safe. I was focused on doing another task at the time and weary of trying to get an invincible teenager to grapple with his mortality.

The moment came back to me the next morning in my Examen. I held up this fragment of a memory—the anxiety, the hesitation, the discomfort—to God and became aware that I felt disconnected from my son. Most of our recent communication centered on rules and commands. He went to school and work, and when he was home, I was telling him to clean his room, brush his teeth, take a shower, do his homework, and let out the dogs.

I ignored his blatant disregard for our rules because I didn't want to push him further away. The awareness led to a request to show me other ways to be with my son. Other opportunities to have fun with him or experience something with him. I also asked for strength to be the parent in the relationship.

And then I took a minute to fathom the kindness of God that allows me to consider what I really want in a relationship with my child. To fathom the gentle reminder that parenting often involves uncomfortable encounters with your child and that I am enough for them. To fathom the creative heart of God that looks for ways to love us all.

A few ordinary minutes of my day led to an important discovery and connection with God. The awareness, once seen with God's eyes, felt huge to me. This regular moment led to a big revelation and change in direction. It also counts if your moment was seeing a red cardinal and feeling seen or washing the dishes and experiencing gratitude for running water and other creature comforts. The point isn't the size of the revelation but where you choose to put what you notice. Can you place the fragments of your day before God and fathom what God has done?

ALL THE MORE

- Today, as you pray the Examen, imagine yourself, like Nancy, with a basket collecting the fragments of your day. Put in the basket anything that comes up for you when you ask to see your day through God's eyes.

- Use the words fragment and fathom as a breath prayer. As you breathe in, say the word "fragment." As you breathe out, say the word "fathom." Repeat that four or five times.

- As a memory or image surfaces from your day, ask God to show you presence, love, goodness, and hope in it.

day 3: movement

"I find the great thing in this world is not so much where we stand, as in what direction we are moving: To reach the port of heaven, we must sail sometimes with the wind and sometimes against it—but we must sail, and not drift, nor lie at anchor."
— OLIVER WENDELL HOLMES

Consolation and desolation are core concepts within Ignatian Spirituality. Ignatius "discovered" them while recuperating from his catastrophic war injury. Here is Ignatius in his own words (note that he uses the third person when referring to himself):

Still, there was this difference: that when he was thinking about that worldly stuff he would take much delight, but when he left it aside after getting tired, he would find himself dry and discontented. But when about going to Jerusalem barefoot, and about not eating except herbs, and about doing all the other rigours he was seeing the saints had done, not only used he to be consoled while in such thoughts, but he would remain content and happy even after having left them aside. But he wasn't investigating this, nor stopping to ponder this difference, until one time when his eyes were opened a little, and he began to marvel at this difference in kind and to reflect on it, picking it up from experience that from some thoughts he would be left sad and from others happy, and little by little coming to know the difference in kind of spirits that were stirring: the one from the devil, and the other from God. (From the *Reminiscences* of St Ignatius of Loyola)[11]

This was the first reflection he made on the things of God; and later, when he produced the Exercises, it was from here that he began to get clarity regarding the matter of the difference in kind of spirits.

St. Ignatius is known for his writings on discernment, which are found all through the Spiritual Exercises and inextricably bound up in them. The process of discernment, as he understood it, involves sorting out people and situations and then moving, based on that knowledge, in the direction of faith, hope, and love. Another way to understand it is that a person with discernment makes good decisions and acts on them.

Ignatius believed that the forces of good and evil vied for our attention as we made decisions. The "discernment of spirits" is what Ignatius called the approach of telling good and evil apart. He further taught that you should pay attention to the interior movements of the soul, which include your feelings, thoughts, desires, imaginings, repulsions, and attractions in order to tell the difference. You would be ready to make the right choice once

11   Elias O. Opongo and A. E. Orobator, *Faith Doing Justice* (Kenya: Paulines Publications Africa, 2008), 16.

you'd noticed, reflected on, understood, and listened to all of these movements in God's presence.

Ignatius used the Examen as the source for much of the information he gathered for the discernment of spirits. The Examen reveals the interior movements (or "motions of the soul" as he named it) day by day.

The *movement* Ignatius was interested in was a person's felt experience of moving toward God or away from God—toward good or toward evil. The assumption is that God never moves. God is always near. The discernment is not about whether God is near or far but whether you *feel* as though God is near or far from you. Ignatius understood that our awareness of God shifts and our movement toward or away from God fluctuates. We feel as though we move—God doesn't. A feeling (sadness, fear, anger) leads us to experience God as near or far—the same with a thought or desire.

It wasn't the motions of the soul themselves he was after but the direction those movements caused a person to go. The words he used to better clarify the direction of our souls were **consolation** and **desolation**.

Even if you've never heard the words consolation and desolation, you're probably familiar with what they mean. Have you ever heard someone say they have a peace about a decision or situation they are in? That is consolation. On the other hand, when someone says they have no peace about a decision, that is desolation.

James Martin says, "If you are in accord with God's presence within you, you will feel a sense of rightness, of peace, what Ignatius called 'consolation' It is an indication that you are on the right path."[12] Martin further details how desolation is the opposite

---

12   James Martin, SJ, *The Jesuit Guide to (Almost) Everything: A Spirituality for Real Life* (New York: HarperOne, 2012), 308.

of consolation. You feel completely listless, tepid, unhappy, and separated from God—signaling that you are on the wrong path.

Over the years, I've accumulated a treasure trove of wisdom about consolation and desolation that helps me discern if my interior movements are moving me toward God or away from God. I find these pairings invaluable to discerning one from the other.

- Consolation = I am present, connected. | Desolation = I am detached, medicated.
- Consolation = I believe Jesus is with me. | Desolation = I believe I am alone.
- Consolation = Warm like a fire. | Desolation = Cold like a black hole.
- Consolation = I feel an emotion appropriate to the situation. | Desolation = I feel an emotion inappropriate to the situation (under- or overreaction).
- Consolation = Every increase of faith, hope, and love. | Desolation = Opposite of faith, hope, and love—like darkness of soul, disturbance, movement to things low and earthly, disquiet, agitations, and temptations.

It's important to say here that Ignatius taught that all of life is the ebb and flow of consolation and desolation. Everyone goes through both every day, every year. They are a normal part of the spiritual life. Consolation and desolation can refer to the current season of your life or to specific experiences or moments that drew you toward or away from God.

> All of life is the ebb and flow of consolation and desolation.

Much like the high/low exercise at dinner, the Examen often highlights for you your consolations (moments that brought you to God) and your desolations (moments that drew you away from God). For example, let's say you remember, in your Examen, your friend calling and sharing good news with you. You notice jealousy, then your guilt over your jealousy as you reflect on the call. You become aware of the ungenerous thoughts you harbored about your friend for a good portion of the day. All of these are moments of desolation.

As you continue the review of your day, you remember taking a walk and observing the new growth on the trees lining your street. The buds reminded you that newness returns each year and invited you to ponder the faithfulness of God. This is a moment of consolation.

When you get to the gratitude and forgiveness portion of the Examen, you thank God for your walk (and all it taught you) and confess your stingy heart about your friend. You ask for help and move on. Most people have multiple moments of consolation and desolation each day. The Examen is so helpful in keeping track of the general direction of your day—toward God or away from God.

Seasons of consolation and desolation look a little different. You have less control over seasons. A season of consolation is experienced as a gift. No matter what happens, your overall sense is that God is near and all is well. Hard things happen, difficult emotions crop up, but your thoughts remain focused on faith, hope, and love.

Without warning, you enter a different season (desolation) and find that you struggle to see God. Faith, hope, and love seem far from you, and nothing you do brings you out of your funk.

The most important thing to know here is that this is normal. Everybody goes through times like this. It doesn't mean God has abandoned you (desolation) or that you've got this life thing figured out (consolation). Whatever you are experiencing will eventually give way to something new.

In her book *Inner Compass*, Margaret Silf provides gobs of excellent information about consolation and desolation. Here, she outlines the common characteristics of each:

Consolation
- directs our focus outside and beyond ourselves.
- lifts our hearts so that we can see the joys and sorrows of other people.
- bonds us more closely to our human community.
- generates new inspiration and ideas.
- restores balance and refreshes our inner vision.
- shows us where God is active in our lives and where he is leading us.
- releases new energy in us.
- causes us to feel drawn toward something.

Desolation
- turns us in on ourselves.
- drives us down the spiral ever deeper into our own negative feelings.
- cuts us off from community.
- makes us want to give up on things that used to be important to us.
- takes over our whole consciousness and crowds out our distant vision.
- covers up all our landmarks.
- drains us of energy.
- causes us to feel driven.[13]

---

13 Margaret Silf, *Inner Compass: An Invitation to Ignatian Spirituality* (Chicago: Loyola Press, 2007), 84–85.

Ponder your last twenty-four hours. Do you recognize any moments of consolation? A desire to check on a grieving friend, the willingness to seek conflict resolution, the presence of a new, exciting idea, a response to God's leading, the awareness that you are enough? However brief or small, any moment that draws you closer to God (faith, hope, and love) is worth giving thanks for and remembering. Write them down. Cherish each one. You will need them in desolation.

Do you recognize any moments of desolation? A lack of God's felt presence, incapability of moving out of your own pain, a focus only on what could go wrong, the desire to hide or isolate, a resentment in helping someone else? Tiny moments of desolation, when added up, lead to seasons of darkness and hopelessness. Be vigilant. Reach out—even when it's the last thing you want to do. Pull out your journal and remember when God felt close and you felt loved.

Ignatius wrote copious rules for discerning the direction your soul is taking. I've found many of his discernment rules helpful in making decisions in my own life. It's possible he's the originator of (my favorite) the pro/con list! For our purposes, I want to keep to general principles of what to do when you notice consolations and desolations in the Examen. Margaret Silf again offers the rules in accessible language.

In Consolation:
1. Tell God how you feel and thank Him.
2. Store this moment in your memory to return to when things get tough. Writing it down always helps.
3. Add this experience to your [story with God].
4. Use the energy you feel to further your deepest desires.

5. Let the surplus energy fuel the things you don't like doing and do them.
6. Welcome the experience of consolation.
7. Go back to 1.

In Desolation:
1. Tell God how you feel and ask for help.
2. Seek out companionship.
3. Don't make life-changing decisions and don't go back on decisions you made in consolation.
4. Stand still and remember [who you are].
5. Recall a time of consolation and go back to it in your imagination.
6. Look for someone who needs your help and turn your attention toward them.
7. Be on guard.
8. Go back to 1.[14]

You don't have control over which way your soul leans from one moment to the next. Just as you don't control what feelings or thoughts pop up for you in any given circumstance.

Faithfulness looks like:
- Own what you become aware of.
- Offer it to God.
- Take the next right step.

When you pray the Examen and discern a moment or season of consolation, give thanks—you didn't earn it and you don't deserve it. It is a gift. Keep a record of it and use it to do what you

---

14   Silf, *Inner Compass: An Invitation to Ignatian Spirituality*, 105.

know you are called to do—love the people around you, serve the poor, do your work. (I do recommend cleaning out the garage, filing your paperwork, or repainting the bedroom in consolation—sooo much extra energy!)

The same applies to moments and seasons of desolation. There is nothing wrong with you. You don't deserve it. You can't fix it. Own it. Tell God about it. And do the next right thing. Call a good friend. Ask them to remind you of the faith, hope, and love they see in your life. Practice Psalm 42:6, "When my soul is in the dumps, I rehearse everything I know of you." Get out of your bed, your house, and help someone else. Remember that drivenness will only further desolation. Let go and trust that God will move you and has not abandoned you.

A final word on consolation and desolation is that they are contagious. Be aware of yourself in a group, in your family, or at work. You know what it's like to ride the wave of another's joy or wither in the presence of another's bad mood. A loving response when you are in consolation is to share your feelings with others (without being annoying), use the energy for good, and be thankful. In desolation, however, give your feelings to God (and a good friend)—spreading them around won't help you or anyone else—and turn your attention away from yourself and toward others. Bless your community in consolation and receive from your community in desolation.

ALL THE MORE

- Name a season of consolation for you. Name a season of desolation. Go back over the list of characteristics for each one. What resonates with your experience?
- Most of us tend to gravitate naturally toward one kind of pathway—consolation or desolation. We have other words for it: optimist/pessimist; positive/ negative; glass half-full/half-empty; Tigger/Eeyore. Know your tendencies and challenge yourself to look for what you often miss.
- God is near. God never moves. Do you operate out of this mentality? How would it change things for you if you did?

day 4: waiting

"Some people seem to understand this—that life and change take time—but I am not one of those people."
— ANNE LAMOTT

Have you ever had to wait for an answer from God? Really wait? The kind of waiting that happens over weeks and months or even years for a direction, a release, an awareness, a change. I'm the worst at waiting. I don't do well at long traffic lights, and I purposely drive routes that do not require me to wait at the longest ones. I sigh dramatically when I pull up to the drive-through pharmacy or the grocery check-out and more than one person is in front of me.

I wonder if I don't wait well because I haven't been taught to value the process. I often believe that to wait is to do nothing. Or that waiting causes me to miss out on life. Worse still is my belief that if God doesn't fix what is broken right away, then there must be something wrong with me and my faith—or God. Waiting exposes my fears. And fears are scary.

Sue Monk Kidd asks, "How did we ever get the idea that God would supply us on demand with quick fixes, that God is merely a rescuer and not a midwife?" I like to imagine God as a midwife because it immediately requires that I accept a period of waiting. Both of my pregnancies seemed to last a loooong time (especially the one when I was nine months pregnant in a Tennessee August) and the labors themselves took time. I didn't like the waiting, but I learned throughout pregnancy and childbirth that good things happen in the dark. Growth happens even when I'm not watching.

In the last couple of months, I've been baking sourdough bread. A friend gave me a starter, a sheet of instructions, and a promise that this twenty-five-year-old starter is forgiving and hardy. In other words, I couldn't mess it up.

If you've never made bread, you need to know it takes a while. After mixing the ingredients into a bowl and feeding the starter, eight hours must pass before the next step. After the initial wait, dough is placed in bread pans to rise. Another eight hours. Sixteen hours after I start the process, I can bake my bread.

The practice of baking bread has been good for me. (Eating bread, on the other hand, may not be good for me, but it fills me with more joy than I can describe. There is nothing like toasted homemade bread with enough butter on it to drip down every side. Heaven.) It reminds me that there is work to be done that I cannot do. The yeast in the bread is like the Spirit in my soul— working in the dark for my good. When you wait, you are "allowing your soul to grow up. If you can't be still and wait, you can't become what God created you to be."[15]

The Examen is God's mercy to me while I wait. As the Spirit accomplishes what only the Spirit can, I continue to notice the daily graces that come my way. I may not receive the answer or

---

the freedom I wait for today, but I can be aware of God's presence and attention. Kidd further writes, "You can't control the life in you. It grows and emerges in its own time. Be patient and nurture it with all your love and attentiveness. Be still and cooperate with the mystery God is unfolding in you. *Let it be.*"[16]

Waiting so often causes forgetfulness in me. I don't remember that God is faithful or loving to me. I forget that God has it—that the timing is as it should be. When I notice the daily graces in my life, I'm reminded of God's love for me. As Paulo Coelho says, "Why is patience so important? Because it makes us pay attention." Examen brings me back to the truth of my life and gives me patience to wait.

I've read the following letter from a Jesuit priest to his niece regularly since a friend shared it with me almost ten years ago. I hope it helps you be still and wait.

Patient Trust, by Teilhard de Chardin, SJ

Above all, trust in the slow work of God. We are quite naturally impatient in everything to reach the end without delay. We would like to skip the intermediate stages. We are impatient of being on the way to something unknown, something new.

And yet, it is the law of all progress that it is made by passing through some stages of instability —and that it may take a very long time.

---

16 Monk Kidd, 111.

And so I think it is with you; your ideas mature gradually—let them grow, let them shape themselves, without undue haste. Don't try to force them on, as though you could be today what time (that is to say, grace and circumstances acting on your own good will) will make of you tomorrow.

Only God could say what this new spirit gradually forming in you will be. Give our Lord the benefit of believing that his hand is leading you, and accept the anxiety of feeling yourself in suspense and incomplete.

ALL THE MORE

- What does your impatience look like on a daily basis?
- How do you "force" ideas to mature or grow?
- "Give the benefit of the doubt" is a common saying. What new meaning does it take on when applied to how you see God's activity in your life?
- Living in the tension of waiting is hard. How can you be kind to yourself in the process?

day 5: gratitude

"If the only prayer you said was thank you,
that would be enough."
— MEISTER ECKHART

My mom has a small, needlepoint sign in her bathroom that reads, "There is always, always, always, something to be grateful for." I see it most times I go to visit. It's been hanging in some version of her bathroom for the better part of twenty years. My perspective on gratitude has evolved, along with my mom's bathroom decor, but the truth of that statement remains the same.

I read the book *One Thousand Gifts* by Ann Voskamp the same year I did the Spiritual Exercises. I was a jumble of ideas and beliefs—halfway between doctrine and rules and contemplation and presence. What I remember about reading the book is that something beautiful in it was drawing me to God, even as my drive to do the right thing (be grateful) was pulling me away.

I've said over the years that gratitude was my favorite whipping tool. Self-flagellation was a popular practice among eleventh-century monks who wanted to discipline themselves to obey. My efforts to practice gratitude weren't nearly as gruesome but no less intense. When I caught myself feeling sad, hurt, or angry, I forced myself to recall something for which I could be grateful. It was my very flawed way of not letting my feelings take over. There was no joy in my gratitude, only faithfulness.

Still, I could sense the beauty in the practice of gratitude even if I couldn't understand it quite yet. And slowly, as I practiced the Examen and other forms of prayer in the Exercises, something shifted in my relationship to gratitude. I gave room to let all the things be present before God—the good, the bad, and the ugly. As I sat with the bad and the ugly and didn't try to deny, ignore or repress it, the good grew larger—no longer diminished by the bad or used by the ugly for an antidote. The graces and gifts of my day opened me up to God in a new way, and I delighted in giving thanks for each one.

I like the way Thomas Merton says it:

> To be grateful is to recognize the Love of God in everything He has given us—and He has given us everything. Every breath we draw is a gift of His Love, every moment of existence is a grace, for it brings with it immense graces from Him. Gratitude therefore takes nothing for granted, it is never unresponsive, is constantly awakening to new wonder and to praise of the goodness of God. For the grateful person knows that God is good, not by hearsay but by experience. And that is what makes all the difference.

I recognized that I was taking gifts for granted. That even in using gratitude as a whipping tool, I was assuming that God would keep supplying them. God is generous inside and out, and gift-giving is the essence of God's character. God does in fact keep giving. God knows no other way. But my way of receiving was not moving me closer to God but further away. Love alone unwrapped the joy of gratitude for me—Love is what makes all the difference.

The graces and gifts of God are hard to spot in the moment. You might be surrounded by people or preoccupied with a task. It's only later, when you go back and reflect, that you can name the sunlight through the window, the soft fur of your dog, the ripeness of the strawberry as a gift. And going back is precisely why the Examen helps you notice the gifts of your day and cultivate a heart of gratitude.

Luke 17 tells the story of Jesus who, on his way to Jerusalem, meets ten lepers who ask for mercy. Jesus takes one look at them and says, "Go, show yourselves to the priests." All turned to go and, as they walked, they were healed. "One of them, when he realized that he was healed, turned around and came back, shouting his gratitude, glorifying God. He kneeled at Jesus's feet, so grateful. He couldn't thank him enough." Jesus wondered aloud where the other nine were—wondered why they hadn't returned. Finally, Jesus says to the one, "Rise and go; your faith has made you well." (NIV)

I love this story. All the lepers did was ask and Jesus gave them everything they needed. He is just that openhanded. Unaccustomed to such generosity, the ten walked off. I picture mayhem when they all realized they were healed. Can you imagine this motley band of misfits seeing themselves and their friends healed and whole? They must have whooped and yelled and smacked each other on the back. I bet they made plans for what they wanted to do first now that they would be allowed back into society. The noise would have been deafening.

No wonder nine of them got distracted and didn't return to give thanks. But one did. He went back and kneeled at Jesus' feet.

He saw the gift for what it was. He couldn't thank him enough. And only he heard Jesus speak to him, encourage him, and commission him to go.

This is really what you miss out on when you don't go back and give thanks for the gifts of your days. It makes sense that you forget in the moment. But when you go back, you get Jesus. You get more generosity, more care, more love. Why would you want to miss that?

James Martin, SJ, tells the story of leading a group of actors through the Examen as part of their summer workshop. One of the actors confessed to having a hard time meditating or believing in God. After praying the Examen, though, he said, "I never knew that my yesterday was so beautiful."[17] That's what we get when we go back and give thanks in the Examen—the awareness of the beauty with which God graces our lives.

---

17   Martin, *The Jesuit Guide to (Almost) Everything: A Spirituality for Real Life*, 101.

ALL THE MORE

- The good/bad, hard/easy, flow/stuck of your life is not an equation. One doesn't negate the other or balance the other or take from the other. Try to let all the things exist together in your recollection of the day. Notice if the good tastes sweeter when you mix all the ingredients together.

- Is there something you want to go back and thank God for after reading about the ten lepers? Don't be shy. Go back and make a scene with thanks to God.

- The First Principle and Foundation says this, "All the things in this world are gifts of God, presented to us so that we can know God more easily and make a return of love more readily." Another Ignatian motto is "All is gift." Does this motto challenge you? Feel like an invitation? Make you curious about a person, situation, or event in your life?

- Pay attention to the moments of consolation that rise as you review your day. See if you can pick out three things to give thanks for each day in your Examen.

day 6: feelings

"There's no 'should' or 'should not' when it comes to having feelings. They're part of who we are and their origins are beyond our control. When we can believe that, we may find it easier to make constructive choices about what to do with those feelings."
— FRED ROGERS

Very early on in the Spiritual Exercises, my spiritual director asked us to think through our own understanding of feelings and silence. We were encouraged to consider the messages—spoken and unspoken—that we internalized about each.

I came up with three main ideas about feelings—all of which were negative:

1. Don't be too sensitive. It's not always about you. Feelings are self-focused and, therefore, bad and selfish (bless this Enneagram One's heart again—I saw everything as bad and selfish).

2. They are not the point and, therefore, not helpful. You need to do what you need to do, and feelings don't help you do that.

3. They are scary because they may not be acknowledged, and they may cause people to withdraw from you.

I ended up with two main ideas about silence—one negative and one positive:

1. Silence is scary because it keeps me from knowing what another person is thinking, and I may be caught off guard by the truth of it when it comes out.
2. I need silence to really think.

I need silence to really think. Thank God for this gift gently laid in front of me while I'm busy looking at everyone else. Not only did this awareness move the focus from others back to me, but it also shifted the purpose of silence from "the right thing to do" to an invitation. I hadn't yet considered that silence is nourishing and healing. I thought of it mostly in terms of another person's silence. And most of my thoughts about feelings centered on other people's feelings, not on my own emotions. That girl had a lot to learn, and the Examen helped (helps!) me do it.

I began noticing my feelings as I went through my day in the Examen, and I was surprised by how much was there. Letting my emotions surface was scary and hard. Laying them out before God seemed silly and pointless to me at first.

I resisted the whole thing until one morning when I could not escape the awareness that I felt hurt—by God (He wasn't working things out like I wanted) and by people I loved. I felt my hurt from my head to my toes and wept from the pain and depth of it. Stories of Jesus feeling hurt flooded my memory—when the disciples fell asleep while he was praying, when he was misunderstood, when he cried out to God from the cross—and I knew in that moment that he understood how I felt.

Jesus not only understood but offered healing for my hurt. I didn't know (really know) before then that my emotions could bring me intimacy with God. More than that, I didn't know that engaging my feelings would awaken deeper love for Jesus—and greater compassion for myself.

The Examen changed my relationship with my own emotions. I always had feelings; I just didn't know what to do with them. They leaked out when I least expected it and morphed into darker versions of themselves when I ignored them. Within the safe bubble of the Examen, I could bring them out to play—to be seen, to be cared for, to be heard. "It seems surprising (and somewhat risky) to trust our feelings to the degree Ignatius does....but [Ignatius] tells us that we live in a world that is permeated by God, a world God uses to keep in touch with us. We seek to follow Jesus. We carefully observe him in the Gospels....We come to know who Jesus is and strive to make him the center of our lives. We make our decisions within the context of this relationship of love. It is a relationship of the heart. The heart will tell us which decisions will bring us closer to Jesus and which will take us away from him....as long as the heart has been schooled by Christ."[18]

Not for the first time, I'm so grateful I get to grow and evolve in my understanding of something. With many thanks to spiritual directors, counselors, books, and teachers, here's the framework I use today to think about feelings:

- Feelings are neutral energies, essential to and normal to the human experience, that reside in the body. I can locate where in my body I'm experiencing my feelings (e.g., chest, stomach, head, back), name them, and care for them.

---

18 Fleming, *What Is Ignatian Spirituality?*, 93.

- Feelings create movement one way or another. I can allow my feelings, however difficult, to move me toward God.
- I can feel many things at one time.
- Feelings aren't facts, but they are information. If I consistently feel a particular emotion, I can learn something about myself or a situation I'm in by paying attention to it.
- I can take time to notice my feelings and feel my feelings.
- I can choose to tell the truth about my feelings. Hiding or suppressing them doesn't make them less true or go away.
- I'm invited to be with God in my feelings.
- I can let myself be loved in my feelings.

My first spiritual director, Renee, offered this feelings chart soon into my journey with the Spiritual Exercises. I've been using it ever since. Different versions exist of this chart (every spiritual director I know has added or subtracted some element of it!), but this basic one helps me understand what I'm experiencing and make sense of what I'm feeling.[19]

---

19   Chart credit to Renee Farkas, Brené Brown, Chip Dodd, and Fr. Dick Hauser.

FEELINGS
Recognizing Internal Movements

Movement Toward Lack of Faith, Hope and Love		Movement Toward Greater Faith, Hope and Love
Depression/ Revenge	**ANGER**	Passion/ Healthy Boundaries
Anxiety/Control/ Rage	**FEAR**	Trust/Confidence/ Wisdom
Resentment	**HURT**	Courage/Seek Help/ Forgive
Apathy/Boredom/ Tired	**LONELY**	Intimacy/ Connection
Self-Pity	**SAD**	Acceptance/ Honor Loss
Paranoia	**GUILT**	Freedom

(Regret of things done/left undone—What I do)

Inadequacy/ Hubris	**SHAME**	Humility/Empathy/ Knowing Own Limits

(Pervasive feeling that I am not enough—Who I am)

Indulgence/ Cynicism	**GLAD**	Hope/Joy/ Generosity

The middle words (anger, hurt, lonely, etc.) are generally acknowledged to be the eight core emotions humans experience. All emotions (confused, annoyed, tired, jealous, etc.) have, at the root, one of these eight core emotions.

The words on the left side help describe what you might be aware of first. You might not know you are lonely (for time with yourself, for another person, or for God), but you may sense that you are bored or lack the energy to do *anything*. Identifying bored or apathetic allows you to wonder if lonely is what is really going on inside of you.

The words on the right side help describe what might come after you've held your core feeling out to God and asked for healing and help. A movement toward faith, hope, and love when you are lonely is to reach out to God or to a trusted confidant. You want intimacy and connection. Feeling lonely is your sign that you are lacking what you are made for.

Your goal isn't to pray a feeling away but to pray with the feeling—instead of "God, take away my loneliness," try "God, show me whatever I need to see about you or myself IN my loneliness. Open up a path toward you IN my loneliness." As you tell the truth about the feeling and receive God's care in it, you move closer to faith, hope, and love. When you deny or judge the feeling, you tend to move further away from faith, hope, and love.

The Voice of the Heart by Chip Dodd and *Emotionally Healthy Spirituality* by Peter Scazzero are two great resources for exploring emotions.

ALL THE MORE

- Offer thanks for God's presence with you, no matter what you are feeling.
- Ask for the Spirit's help in seeing whatever emotion is present to you in this moment.
- Review your day, paying particular attention to your feelings. When did I feel strong emotions today? When did I experience joy? When was I angry? What scared me? When was I sad?
- Invite Jesus to be with you in your emotions. Let yourself feel his love for you as you experience them.
- Ask for the courage and honesty to tell the truth about your feelings again tomorrow.
- Write a poem in response to a feeling you identify. Express your feelings through any creative medium that helps you gather what's in your heart.

day 7: ish

"Nothing that is worth doing can be achieved in our lifetime;
therefore we must be saved by hope. Nothing which is true or
beautiful or good makes complete sense in any immediate context
of history; therefore we must be saved by faith. Nothing we do,
however virtuous, can be accomplished alone; therefore we are
saved by love."

— Reinhold Niebuhr

Many years ago, at the Nashville Frothy Monkey, I huddled with two dear girlfriends and a shared mentor. I met my girlfriends in grade school and college, and we met Steve Garber through our husbands' non-profit, Blood:Water. Steve writes and speaks about the intersection of faith, vocation, and culture, and that day he spoke to my girlfriends and me about proximate justice. We leaned in closely as he quietly repeated the idea, "It's not everything, but it's not nothing. It's something."

My idealistic mind barely wrapped itself around what he was getting at. My thinking went some-

> "It's not everything, but it's not nothing. It's something."

thing like this—I expect, I work, I work harder, I fail, I quit—and the idea that something is better than nothing did not fit. My brain nearly short-circuited at the introduction of a third way.

Steve talked about the now-but-not-yet nature of the Kingdom—where Jesus already made all things new and yet the reality is hidden from us. He said:

> The only way forward is to make peace with proximate justice. It is a choice to make peace with something, something that is honest and true, something that is more just and more merciful, even if it is not everything. All-or-nothing never works—in marriages, in friendships, in the workplace, in the church.[20] Proximate justice realizes that something is better than nothing. It allows us to make peace with some justice, some mercy, all the while realizing that it will only be in the new heaven and new earth that we find all our longings finally fulfilled, that we will see all of God's demands finally met. It is only then—there we will see all of the conditions for human flourishing finally in place, socially, economically, and politically.[21]

I failed to grasp the extent of what he was saying in the moment, but that phrase stuck with me. I started using it when my ideals collapsed, but a small grace emerged from the rubble that allowed me to keep going. When what I hoped for or worked

---

20   Steven Garber, "Proximate Justice, Again and Again," The Washington Institute, April 26, 2019, https://washingtoninst.org/proximate-justice-again-and-again/.
21   Steven Garber, "Finding Our Way to Great Work, Even in Politics: Making Peace with Proximate Justice," *Comment* magazine, December 1, 2007, https://www.cardus.ca/comment/article/finding-our-way-to-great-work-even-in-politics-making-peace-with-proximate-justice/.

toward didn't materialize, light still found its way in through the cracks. It's not everything, but it's not nothing. It's something.

I say "It's something" unconsciously now about a walk I squeeze in between rainstorms or a new novel by my favorite author released in the midst of a difficult week. The somethings are the graces that I notice each day and, laid out one next to the other, create a path for me to follow toward faith, hope, and love.

A couple of years after that meeting at Frothy Monkey, I joined a delightful group of women for a bible study on Tuesday mornings. Not one of us had it all together, and we called it good if we just got there each week. Months into the study, we named ourselves the "Ish" girls. "Ish" comes from a beautiful children's book by Peter H. Reynolds with the same title.

The book tells the story of Ramon, a frustrated artist who crumples up drawing after drawing because they don't look like he imagines they should. His sister, Marisol, keeps each one and helps him see that his drawings may not look like a vase of flowers, but it looks vase-ish. Ish drawing frees Ramon to create many beautiful pieces of art. He drew ish pictures, ish feelings, and wrote ish poems. In the book, "Ramon lived ishfully ever after."

Ish means "to some extent" and to some extent, the "ish" girls were seeking God, reading the bible, and praying for one another. Life interrupted and trials dulled the desire, but we were trying-ish—we were faithful-ish. Each of us showed up with wounds and questions that did not resolve from one week to the next. We learned to be content with togetherness, with empathy, with effort. Our fearless leader bought us all blue coffee mugs with "ish girls" on it, and we let it be. Each, in our own way, grew more comfortable with ish. We accepted the substantial healing that Francis Schaeffer talks about in *True Spirituality*:[22]

> The alternatives are not between being perfect or being nothing. Just as people smash marriages because they are looking for what is romantically and sexually perfect and in this poor world do not find it, so human beings often smash what could have been possible in a true church or true Christian group. It is not just the "they" involved who are not yet perfect, but the "I" is not yet perfect either. In the absence of present perfection, Christians are to help each other on to increasingly substantial healing on the basis of the finished work of Christ. This is our calling.

Proximate justice, something, "ish," substantial healing—all of it you can uncover in the Examen. If you set your vision on perfection, on flawlessness, or complete peace, your eyes will cross and grow weary. But if you show up ready to see "something," willing to see "substantial healing," then you won't be disappointed.

Ask the Spirit to help you see. Maybe a broken relationship is still miles from restoration, but a text is something. Maybe some bills remain unpaid, but an unexpected financial gift is something. Maybe your mind is flooded with anxiety, but your dog's head on your lap is substantial healing. Whatever it is for you, pay attention to it, thank God for it, and trust God to use it to bring you greater faith, hope, and love.

---

22   Francis A. Schaeffer, *True Spirituality* (Tyndale House Publishers, 2001).

ALL THE MORE

- Identify something honest or true from your day. Something more merciful or more just. Ask God to use it to bring you peace and contentment.
- When you ask God to be with you tomorrow, ask for the hope of a future where everything wrong will be made right. Ask God to show you how to build that kingdom grace by grace in your life now.
- What feels "ish" in your life right now?
- Name a wound that feels raw and sore. Ask God to help you receive the graces that bring healing. Name a problem that has yet to be resolved. Ask God for wisdom to see an "ish" or substantial solution.

day 8: curiosity

"The important thing is not to stop questioning. Curiosity has its own reason for existence. One cannot help but be in awe when he contemplates the mysteries of eternity, of life, of the marvelous structure of reality. It is enough if one tries merely to comprehend a little of this mystery each day."

— Albert Einstein

Curiosity is defined by a strong desire to know or learn something. Maybe you felt it when you saw the title of this book—you wanted to learn something about prayer, the Examen, or God's presence in your everyday life. Curiosity further involves being inquisitive, wondering, ready to poke around and figure something out.[23]

In recent years, curiosity has been linked to happiness, creativity, satisfying intimate relationships, increased personal growth after traumatic experiences, and increased meaning in life. Businesses hire for curiosity and engage in curiosity-building exercises to increase productivity and innovation.

---

23 "Curiosity—Dictionary Definition," Vocabulary.com, https://www.vocabulary.com/dictionary/Curiosity.

For all of its glowing press, it wouldn't seem that there is anything wrong with it. But the word used to mean "very, very careful," and only in the last few hundred years has it turned into a word expressing the desire to know more. A quick Google search of faith and curiosity yields dozens of articles warning Christians away from being curious.

I won't attempt to explain why some Christians fear a strong desire to know or learn something. What I know to do when I'm confused by the beliefs, actions, or thought processes of God's people is to look at God. So, let's look at how Jesus interacts with curious people.

You can't read long in the gospels without running into crowds of people who followed Jesus around and waited to see what he would do and say. These people asked questions, asked for help, and touched his clothes, all in an effort to know something about this man.

Jesus crossed seas and walked miles to provide answers, compassion, and healing. Zacchaeus climbed a tree to get a better look at Jesus, and Jesus responded to him by inviting himself to dinner. Nicodemus sought out Jesus in the middle of the night and Jesus taught him, right then and there, the ways of God. So many of Jesus's words are responses to the questions people asked him. If he didn't like the motive behind the question, Jesus asked one of his own.

Jesus did not shy away from curiosity—in fact, he invited and encouraged it. In Matthew 7:7–8 (ESV), Jesus said, "Ask, and it will be given to you; seek, and you will find; knock, and it will be opened to you. For everyone who asks receives, and the one who seeks finds, and to the one who knocks it will be opened." Ask, seek, and knock—all curious actions. And Jesus is *all in* to meet people there and lead them to greater faith, hope, and love.

The Examen makes good use of the curiosity components of "wondering" and "poking around." When you review your day, you poke through your memories, your feelings, your thoughts, and your questions—all in the hope of seeing God.

You wonder where God has chosen to make faith, hope, and love obvious to you. There is something unhurried about curiosity—something other than a demand to know how the pieces fit or insistence in complete knowledge of a situation.

Curiosity lingers over a moment or a story and asks questions about possible meanings. Over the course of the last few days, I heard the same song on the radio every time I got into the car. I'm not in the car much these days and drive no more than ten minutes at a time. I noted one morning in the Examen that I heard the song two times. When I heard it for the fourth time, the song sparked my curiosity, and I wondered if God had something for me in it—so I looked up the lyrics. The chorus assures the beloved that the lover will walk through fire for her—that the only thing the lover wants to do is adore her.

I should tell you now that I have an incredibly cringe-worthy habit of taking pop music and repurposing it into worship. I look for God in the lyrics of songs I hear on the radio. It isn't a special fondness for Harry Styles then (although he sings one of my favorite lyrics ever about hair flipping as an overwhelming situation) that drove my curiosity but a belief that God is present to me even in music. And, as crazy as it sounds, I needed to hear from God—through a Harry Styles song—that I am adored and championed.

My week had been full of disappointment, inconvenience, and frustration. My normally sunny disposition disappeared and left a grumpy bear that frightened my family. The lines ahead of the chorus let the beloved know that nothing is expected, nothing is needed. Just be adored. Message received. And savored. A grace impossible to receive without the curiosity to wonder if God speaks through pop songs.

Curiosity also disrupts our binary thinking and prepares us for varied and complicated scenarios. Binary thinking is good/bad, right/wrong, either/or, black/white. The largest and most powerful part of your brain loves the idea that this is how the world works. It craves the clarity of a world that unfolds in a straight line. Your brain is happy if there's a plan, and it takes comfort that if we stick to it, everything will be okay. The world doesn't necessarily work that way, though, does it?

Here's how binary thinking might play out when you pray the Examen. In combing through your experiences of the day, if you notice that people reacted favorably to you, problems got solved, and the weather cooperated with your outdoor plans, then you might assume that God is good.

If, on the other hand, your car broke down, the storm knocked out the internet, and no answer to your daily prayer for discernment came (these all happened to me as I was writing this chapter), you might conclude that God is mad, or bad, or indifferent.

Good things = good God. Bad things = bad God. It's an either/or situation with binary thinking. There is no room for curiosity when right or wrong are the only two categories available—we aren't curious about the good because it's what we wanted, and we aren't curious about the "bad" because it creates too much anxiety.

But what if God is up to something more? What if what you perceive is good is blinding you from God's grace in providing. Or what if what you perceive as bad is blinding you from God's comfort in suffering. You won't know until you ask. Get curious. You can trust that God will answer.

> Good things = good God. Bad things = bad God.

ALL THE MORE

- Describe the messages you've received about curiosity. How do you think faith and curiosity relate to one another?
- If you notice yourself lingering over a moment or story or conversation, get curious about it. Ask God to show you what it is that holds your attention.
- Think of a few examples of binary thinking in your own life. How does it affect your experience of God? What do you need from God in this?

day 9: savor

"Beautiful places are not just for the moment, while you are there.
They will become homes for you, spaces of solace and comfort,
where you can close your eyes and go. Nothing you experience will
ever go away. It belongs to you now."
— CHARLOTTE ERIKSSON

I spend as much time as I can in my sunroom. My stepdad and my son built me a hanging daybed for my fortieth birthday, and my mom made the covers for three rows of cozy pillows to place on top. My daybed faces bookshelves and a fireplace mantle where I've placed meaningful objects, pictures, books, and words.

When my eyes come to rest on a particular object, I'm reminded of a moment, season, or event from my past. I choose my items carefully to reflect the times when God has proven loving or faithful to me. For example, on a high shelf is the trail marker for a blue run from a mountain in Colorado. Each time I see the marker, I'm invited to remember a trip I took several years ago.

While I grew up skiing small hills in northwest Pennsylvania (think J-Lift-sized), twenty years passed without skiing before I took a trip with dear friends. I didn't know if I could still do it.

My first (uneventful, upright) pass down the practice hill was exhilarating. You would have thought I won the Olympics by the amount of whooping and hollering I did. I skied down next to my best friend and we were screaming, "Nailed it!" over and over to each other.

I remember feeling more brave with each run, and I decided I was ready for a challenge. The day was forty degrees and sunny—a perfect Colorado day in February. On the lift, my friends and I screamed/sung "Rocky Mountain High" by John Denver, and I felt invincible.

The mountains, the sky, and the snow together formed an intoxicating view more beautiful than anything I'd seen. I exited the lift with newfound confidence and turned to look straight down a scary steep hill. Fear settled in my stomach, and I wondered how this was going to work. I started talking to Jesus and asking for presence and help.

I had resigned myself earlier in the day that every seven-year-old could ski faster than me (without poles!) and I knew I had to take it slow. With one eye toward heaven, I began to make my way down that hill in extremely wide zigzags. Two friends went before me and cheered me on the whole way. It took forever. My thighs burned and my heart raced, but I made it to the bottom without falling. It felt incredible.

I look up at that trail sign, Heavenly Daze, whenever I'm confronted with something new, something I don't know how to do, something that feels bigger than me. I savor the memory of a sunny afternoon in Colorado when God met me on a steep hill and brought me safely to the bottom.

I imagine the confidence and community that I experienced that day and believe I will feel that way again about whatever challenge is in front of me. I savor the reality that I am not alone in this world—God and friends carried me that day and carry me still. I remember the beauty and feel God's presence in the world.

St. Ignatius taught that love consists in mutual communication; that is to say that the lover (God) gives and communicates to the loved one (you), and in turn, the loved one does the same for the lover; each gives to the other. The communication happens in the daily events of our lives. The Examen helps us to pay attention to these moments and receive the love God has for us in them. In turn, we return love to God by our acknowledgment of it and thanksgiving for it.

Some days I struggle to feel God's love for me. All of us have days, weeks, or months when communication with God suffers. On these days, we can remember a moment from the past and savor it to remind our hearts that God's love is with us—even when it feels far away.

Life is hard. Troubling things will happen to you—and to those you love—and you will discover painful things inside of you—confusing thoughts and dark feelings in your inner being. Savoring—a moment, a memory, a nugget, a flicker of light—provides a haven for our souls when we are assailed with interior and exterior difficulties in our daily lives.

Carl Jung said that our hurts make us feel fragmented, and we have need to be "re-membered." When you savor a moment of connection or wholeness in God, you invite the pieces of yourself back home—home to love and friendship with God. You place yourself back in what my spiritual director calls a "love loop" (God communicating with you, you communicating with God). You find new energy to receive and offer love in the concrete happenings of your day.

ALL THE MORE

Use the portion of the Examen when you review your day to bring forward an image or a memory of God's love for you. It might look like this:

- Think about a time when you felt God's love—from today or any day. Ask yourself, where have I been with God? Or where has God been with me? Notice what image comes to mind and thank God for it.

- Tell the story again—to yourself and to God. Let the memory live between the two of you. Engage your senses. What do you remember about how it felt, what you heard and smelled?

- Notice the feelings that come up when you recall the experience of being loved. Recognize the feelings as God here with you now. What is the experience like for you? Tell God about it.

- Savor the questions: "What is it like when God is there with me? What am I like? What is the world like?" Tell God. Then listen for a response. Wait a moment. Offer thanks.

day 10: self-compassion

"A moment of self-compassion can change your entire day. A string
of such moments can change the course of your life."
— CHRISTOPHER K. GERMER

About five years into studying the Enneagram, I came face to face with my own inner critic. Everyone has one—that voice that tells you that you're not doing enough, you aren't enough, it's your fault—and in Enneagram Ones (that's me!), it's dialed up past ten. It was so much a part of my daily life that I didn't even recognize it for what it was. It was the wallpaper in my brain, and I played out the conversations in my head without noticing one of the players.

Nothing kills self-compassion like the inner critic. Kristin Neff, author of *Self-Compassion: The Proven Power of Being Kind to Yourself*, defines self-compassion as treating yourself with the same kindness, support, and care that you would give to someone you love. If you wouldn't say it to your best friend, don't say it to yourself. She further identifies three core components of self-compassion:

- Self-kindness—Be warm and supportive in your self-talk instead of cold and judgmental.
- Imperfection is common—Remember that imperfection is a part of the shared human experience. We all experience the shared suffering of making mistakes and having flaws.
- Mindfulness—Own your suffering. When you ignore, deny, or downplay your pain, you miss the opportunity to give yourself compassion. Problem solving or busyness may avoid the pain for a season, but you lose out on the opportunity to give yourself compassion.

I began to voice the badgering comments of my inner critic to friends and they were shocked by their cruel tone. I would never say to someone else what I was saying to myself. In fact, I'm known for my calm speaking voice and diplomatic words. I'm not a name-caller or a yeller. I tend to assign the most positive interpretation to what others say (for better or worse) so my self-talk was especially startling to me when I saw it clearly.

I think I used self-criticism and self-judgment to motivate myself toward good behavior. Somehow, I thought that if I pushed myself hard enough into shame and self-pity, I could attain my high standards—and God's. I marvel that this was my strategy as it's so obviously a bad one. And one I didn't use with anyone else in my life. I didn't stimulate my kids on to love and good deeds that way. I didn't inspire my husband to help around the house with blame and shame (well almost never).

I kept getting tangled up by how I was treating myself and how it didn't match what I knew about love from Jesus. "You shall love the Lord your God with all your heart and with all your soul and with all your strength and with all your mind, and your neighbor as yourself." (Luke 10:27 [ESV]) Jesus summed up all of God's laws with this one verse. Jesus linked the love of God, others, and self and, in doing so, exposed my self-talk for what it was—brokenness in my relationship with God and myself.

We were made in God's image, and we were made for right relationships with everything else God made. My unkind and judgmental self-talk caused a tear in my relational wholeness and wellness with God and myself, which, according to Lisa Sharon Harper, author of *The Very Good Gospel,* and the ancient Hebrews, is the definition of sin. Yikes! All of a sudden it didn't seem so selfish to be kind to myself (an unspoken message I absorbed in my Southern Christian culture). Kindness toward myself was the path to restored relationships with God, me, and others.

If that isn't enough to make you reevaluate your inner critic, research shows that people who are self-compassionate are less likely to be depressed, anxious, and stressed.

So, I started asking God to show me my self-talk in the Examen. I looked for it in my responses to the circumstances and moments of my day. I noticed that the uglier I was toward myself, the further I felt from God. I noticed that I often mistook my inner critic's voice for God's voice. So, I asked to know the difference. I asked if what my inner critic said to me was true. I asked if my inner critic spoke for God. I confessed my unrelenting judgment as often as I saw it and begged for kindness to replace the never satisfied critic.

I didn't see real change until I started to speak kindly to myself out loud. I don't even want to talk about how weird this sounds—and felt—to do. But I started to pay attention to my soul when I did it. And I noticed that I felt close to God, I felt whole, I felt congruent.

When I prayed the Examen, I could see and hear God's love for me and for others more easily than when I was responding with judgment to all of my actions, thoughts, and feelings. I'm not the only one. I asked my directees about their self-talk and discovered that many people struggled just as much as I did with being kind to themselves. I offered the Examen. One person came back to me and said she could finally hear her inner critic. And awareness led her to a choice in how she spoke to herself. She could choose to replace the inner critic with a loving voice. (At one point, she named her inner critic after a cultural villain and her self-compassionate voice after a cultural hero. What name makes sense for your inner critic? Your self-compassionate voice?)

I remember one experience vividly. In my morning Examen, I identified some fear around a conversation I knew I needed to have. I had a history of diplomatic relations breaking down with this person, and I was dreading the conversation. I asked for help to sit in the fear of talking to an unsafe person and the hurt and sadness I felt over the relationship. I knew who I wanted to be and felt my soul moving toward God in the realization of what I wanted to say.

I said what I needed to say later that day, and it didn't go well. In the past, I experienced great distress in these moments. On this night, as I was washing my face, I looked at myself and said, "I'm so proud of you. You did a very brave and courageous thing today, and it wasn't easy. It didn't go well, and I'm sorry. You said what you wanted to say and chose to be who you wanted to be. Rest well tonight. You've done all you can do." I felt God's nearness, and I experienced wholeness with God and myself. There were still deep

> Rest well tonight. You've done all you can do.

tears in the relationship, but I had done all I could do to repair them. The rest was in God's hands.

You are made in God's image. You are endowed with all of the worth and dignity of your Creator. Go gently with yourself. Speak kindly to yourself. Show love to the one who is loved beyond measure by God. Let all the things in your life today remind you of God's nearness and love. They are God's gifts to you. Notice them and they will be gifts you give yourself.

ALL THE MORE

An Examen for Self-Compassion

- **Presence:** You are near to all whom you have made. Thank you for being with me, especially right now.
- **Enlighten:** Show me how to love myself as You love me. You know how I was made, and you remember I am dust. Show me how to have the same compassion for my limitations and humanity. (Psalm 103:14 [ESV])
- **Ask:** What did I offer my heart today? Did I nurture healthy relationships? Did I take time to celebrate big and small accomplishments? Did I engage in energizing or rejuvenating activities? What did I offer my soul today? Did I spend time in silence, solitude, or stillness? Did I listen to my inner thoughts, feelings, and desires? Did I connect to a community of people who share similar beliefs and ideals? What did I offer my body today? Did I move my body? Did I tend to what's broken or hurting in my body? Did I eat and drink what nourishes my body? Did I give my body rest? What did I offer my mind today? Did what I listened to, read, or watched nourish my mind? Did I seek input that leads me closer to who I want to be?
- **Confess:** I confess the ways I failed to nurture what you have created. I confess the ways I have been unloving toward myself in my words, thoughts, and actions. I confess the ways I have hidden from God's love and care.
- **Look Ahead:** Lead me tomorrow toward greater love and compassion for myself. Lead me tomorrow into deeper gratitude for the gifts in my life. Lead me tomorrow to greater knowledge of Your presence, love, and care.

day 11: boundaries

"No one will listen to us until we listen to ourselves."
— Marianne Williamson

Several years ago, a close friend of mine (the funny, sarcastic one) said to me, "I liked you a lot better before you had boundaries." She was kidding, of course. But a part of her meant it. She has been on the receiving end of my giving for years, and I had just told her no to a request she made for my help. I got it—she was used to me doing more for her. I held my ground though—my own sanity and well-being depended on it.

Here's the thing: I like to help people. More than that, I think helping people is the right thing to do. My personality plus Christian teaching on "love one another" was like a dropped lit match on lighter fluid-soaked dry wood. I thought that all of the "one another" verses (love, serve, accept, be devoted to, give preference to, etc.) meant that I had to give and give no matter what. I thought that saying no and taking care of myself were selfish acts.

I spent my twenties and early thirties doing all the things for all the people. I wouldn't have known a boundary if it smacked me in the face. Eventually, though, my fire burnt out. And without the intensity of the flames to keep me warm, I feel resentful, used, and mistreated.

I needed some help. I found it in the form of boundaries. Brené Brown's definition of a boundary is simple: A boundary is "what's okay and what is not okay." And it's what's okay for me—not what's okay for you (I only have control over my own choices and actions). For example, I'm okay to have a conversation when you are calm. I'm not okay to stay in the conversation if talking turns to screaming (I can't control if another person screams at me; I can only control if I choose to listen to screaming).

Henry Cloud further clarifies what a boundary is: "Boundaries define us. They define what is me and what is not me. A boundary shows me where I end and someone else begins, leading me to a sense of ownership. Knowing what I am to own and take responsibility for gives me freedom." I am not responsible for another person's behavior or choices. I am responsible only for me.

So, a boundary is really just a way to draw emotional and spiritual lines between yourself and others—like a fence around what you are responsible for and what you are not. Think of boundaries more in terms of "No, I won't" versus "No, you can't." Instead of saying to an angry person, "You can't talk to me that way," you can communicate a healthy boundary by saying, "I will not continue this conversation if you insist on yelling or name-calling."

While you have no control over how another chooses to communicate, you *do* have control over whether or not you will listen to their words. Once you discover that you need to set a boundary, be clear about what you want and what others can expect from you. Notice if your resentment and frustration toward others can be traced back to you not being clear about a boundary. Resentment is often a red flag that we have not communicated our boundaries clearly.

At this point, you may be wondering what God thinks about boundaries. I don't presume to know God's every thought on the subject, but I can learn something from what God does. Consider the story of creation in Genesis. Lisa Sharon Harper, in *The Very Good Gospel*, shows us the boundaries God placed for our good in creation.

The first boundary is light. Genesis 1:2 reveals a world formless and empty with darkness covering it. Harper writes, "God does not obliterate the darkness; rather, God names it and limits it—puts boundaries around it."[24] Light is God's boundary for darkness—literally in that there is an end to night and figuratively in that there is an end to our suffering. Light prevails every time.

The second boundary is land. The sea dominated the earth in Genesis 1:9. On the third day, God created land to place a boundary on how far the sea could go. A good thing too as God makes a point to tell us about a monster, created on the fifth day, that lives in the sea. Sea monsters represented to the Babylonians vengeance, loss, and fear. By placing the land as a boundary to the sea, God shows that, "we are not subject to the worst the deep has to offer. Rather, the waters and every creature in them are subject to God."[25]

In both cases, God calls the boundaries good and uses the

Boundaries are good and limit harm.

boundaries for our good. God is limiting the harm that comes to us. (Lisa Sharon Harper outlines the Genesis story brilliantly. The first three chapters are worth the cost of the book.)

---

24   Lisa Sharon Harper, *The Very Good Gospel: How Everything Wrong Can Be Made Right* (Colorado Springs, CO: WaterBrook, 2016), 21.

25   Harper, 23.

With this framework in mind—that boundaries are good and limit harm—ponder anew how boundaries are an important part of self-care. I guard my emotional, physical, and spiritual stamina when I take responsibility for only what is mine.

I free up my emotional energy for loving those in my care, my physical energy for accomplishing what God has given me to do, and my spiritual energy for seeking God's presence and voice in my life.

Parker Palmer says, "Self-care is never a selfish act—it is simply good stewardship of the only gift I have, the gift I was put on earth to offer others. Anytime we can listen to true self and give the care it requires, we do it not only for ourselves, but for the many others whose lives we touch."[26] I steward my own heart and soul when I limit the harm to them through boundaries.

Good research also suggests that when you practice boundaries, you increase your ability to communicate your empathy to others. Empathy is the ability to see the world as another sees it—without judgment and with understanding of the other's feelings. Compassion is empathy in action. Compassion seeks to relieve another's pain, not just feel it. Once your boundaries are clear, there will be more room to express empathy for others.

Brené Brown explains, "…very early on in my work I had discovered that the most compassionate people I interviewed also have the most well-defined and well-respected boundaries. It surprised me at the time, but now I get it. They assume that other people are doing the best they can, but they also ask for what they need and they don't put up with a lot of crap. Compassionate people ask for what they need. They say no when they need to, and

26   Parker Palmer, *Let Your Life Speak: Listening for the Voice of Vocation* (John Wiley & Sons, Inc., 2009).

when they say yes, they mean it. They're compassionate because their boundaries keep them out of resentment."[27]

How do you know what boundaries to set? How do you determine what's okay and not okay? Collect the evidence as you pray the Examen. Get quiet. Identify your emotions. Ask God to show you what you need to see. Notice your resentment. Ask for wisdom to see where you failed to communicate your needs. Pay attention to what gives you life and what drains you so when asked, you can respond with the awareness of how an action will affect you.

Remain faithful in your daily practice of the Examen so that over time you can discern the patterns of your behavior and others that are problematic for you. Trust that God will reveal all that you need to see when you need to see it. God created healthy boundaries around the harm that can come to you—God will show you how to take steps to take care of yourself.

---

27   Brown Brené, *Rising Strong: How the Ability to Reset Transforms the Way We Live, Love, Parent, and Lead* (New York: Random House, 2017).

ALL THE MORE

The Examen for Boundaries

- Thank you, God, for the presence of boundaries in creation. From the beginning, You showed me Your goodness in the limits You placed on the darkness and the sea.

- Holy Spirit, show me how God protected me today with God's own boundaries of mercy and love.

- Walk with me through the moments of my day. Help me be honest as I recount them. Am I aware of any resentment in reflecting on what I did or didn't do today? Did I ask for what I need? If not, why?

- Thank you for the light you gave me today. Thank you for the firm ground beneath my feet. Thank you that darkness and the deep are subject to You. Thank you for the border You've placed around them in Your love for me.

- Forgive me for where I took responsibility for another's behavior or choices today. I did not protect my own emotional, physical, and spiritual stamina. Forgive me for where I wasn't honest with myself and others and didn't communicate what I expect and need in a clear way.

- Give me hope that You will be with me tomorrow and give me everything I need to create healthy boundaries for the day.

day 12: forgiveness

"At the end of life, the wish to be forgiven is ultimately the chief
desire of almost every human being. In refusing to wait; in extending
forgiveness to others now, we begin the long journey of becoming the
person who will be large enough, able enough, and generous enough to
receive, at the very end, that absolution ourselves."
— DAVID WHYTE

Forgiveness. I'm not sure which is harder—to give it or to receive it. I only know that it is at the heart of this whole faith thing, and it is one of the more difficult realities to grasp. I'm going to tell you something embarrassing. When I was in college (and very new to faith), I hung the Ten Commandments above my dorm bed and checked them off each night before I went to bed. That's right—*I checked them off!* As in, I read through each one and absolved myself of any wrongdoing each night after I lived the previous twenty-four hours as a disaster of a college student.

I wanted and needed so badly to be good that I lowered the bar far enough to meet the requirements of each commandment. I had no idea what the first two meant beyond saying God's name in vain so, I reasoned, if I didn't cuss, I nailed it. I didn't study or write papers on Sundays (except for a few times) so checked the box for the third. I didn't yell at my parents—check. I didn't murder anyone or cheat on my boyfriend—check, check. I didn't steal (anything that mattered!) so I was good on the seventh. I justified any "little white lies" in such a way that I fulfilled the eighth. I didn't consider myself the jealous type so that covered the last two.

I look back on that girl in college with deep compassion and see her fear and shame. I didn't yet know how loved I was by God, and I couldn't possibly carry my darkness without sinking under the weight of it. I remember how much I disliked when others used the phrase "miss the mark" to refer to my sins (frankly, I didn't like the word sin either—too harsh). What was I missing? Did that mean something was wrong with me? How will I know the mark? Will the mark change in different circumstances?[28]

Five years after college I heard a sermon series on the ten commandments and tried very hard to hide under my chair. The *spirit* of the commandments is far deeper and wider than my literal translation that (with some creative license, I admit) allowed me to be blameless. At the time, I was only wading in the shallow waters of God's love for me and understanding their true meaning was still far off.

My next steps were to do more, be better, and work harder. I latched onto the idea that it is the mark of a mature person to

---

28 Interestingly, the Greeks used an ancient archery term that means "to miss the mark of perfection" to define sin. That translation, combined with the Greek focus on the individual, formed the evangelical understanding of sin. Evangelicals see sin as a failure to be perfect in our outward behavior—we miss the mark in what we do and say. The Hebrews defined sin as anything that undercuts the wholeness and wellness of the relationships God called good in creation. Idea from pp. 47–48 of *The Very Good Gospel: How Everything Wrong Can be Made Right* by Lisa Sharon Harper.

admit their wrongs and ask for forgiveness. So, I admitted them in spades—even things I wasn't responsible for! I hung out there for a number of years.

As I began to grow in intimacy with God, my resistance to my flawed humanity lessened. Of course, I made mistakes. All humans do. I started tiptoeing around the concept of forgiveness with interest and curiosity. Can I still be loved if I'm wrong? Will people love me if they know I'm not perfect?

The Enneagram made all the difference to me as I began to see that my personality was driving so many of these questions focused on my goodness. Once I realized I was letting my ego (or personality) lead, and not my true self, I could be curious about what I needed to let go of to be more loving, faithful, and hopeful. I could wonder what I could add to be better able to know and give love.

Over the course of my year in the Spiritual Exercises, our spiritual director would offer our group different interpretations or versions of the prayer of Examen. The wording of one of them struck a nerve with me as I pondered a new way to see forgiveness. In this version of the Examen, the section on forgiveness centered on asking for healing for the ways I wandered today from God's love.

God, let me be grateful and ask forgiveness.

I thank you for all of the gifts of this day.

I ask for healing and forgiveness for the times today when I wandered from your love.

I knew myself to be a wanderer from love. I sang it with deep feeling, hand to heart, in church—"Prone to wander, Lord I feel it. Prone to leave the God I love."[29] And I sensed the invitation in the request for healing.

---

29   Robert Robinson, composer. "Come Thou Fount of Every Blessing." 1758.

I began to imagine that there was hope for me out here in the wilderness and a warm fire waiting for me in God's love. I started to settle into a more generous belief about forgiveness not unlike what Barbara Brown Taylor describes as "God's cure for the deformity our resentments cause us. It is how we discover our true shape, and every time we do it, we get to be a little more alive."[30] A little more alive and a little more in love.

Over the years, I discovered various translations of the Examen and each remakes the part on forgiveness. James Martin, SJ, labels the forgiveness portion of the Examen "Sorrow." He offers these words: "You may have sinned today or done something you regret. Express your sorrow to God and ask for forgiveness."

Another way is to focus on facing shortcomings as the pathway to healing and restoration. "I face up to what is wrong in my life and in me."[31] Forgiveness is also described as a response to seeing the presence of God in our individual moments. When we notice God in them, we can see what doesn't fit. What doesn't belong. And we can ask for forgiveness.

As I began to grow more comfortable receiving forgiveness, I noticed that my heart found more room to forgive others as well. Richard Rohr, in his CD *The Art of Letting Go*, makes the connection this way, "Forgiveness is of one piece. Those who give it can also receive it. Those who receive it can pass forgiveness on. You are a conduit, and your only job is not to stop the flow."

I found a series of meditations on the Syrian Aramaic version of the Lord's Prayer that further helped me connect God's forgiveness of me with my forgiveness of others. You probably say, "Forgive us our sins, as we forgive those who sin against us." Here

---

30 Barbara Brown Taylor, *Gospel Medicine* (Cambridge, MA: Cowley Publications, 1995), 14.

31 Jim Manney, *A Simple, Life-Changing Prayer* (Loyola Press, 2011).

are a few other possible translations of the petition on forgiveness, based on various connotations of the Aramaic words Jesus might have spoken:

> Loose the cords of mistakes binding us, as we release the strands we hold of others' guilt.

> Lighten our load of secret debts as we relieve others of their need to repay.

> Forgive our hidden past, the secret shames, as we consistently forgive what others hide.[32]

When I consider these translations and think about forgiveness toward others, I'm reminded of Jesus's words in Matthew 11:28–30. "Are you tired? Worn out? Burned out on religion? Come to me. Get away with me and you'll recover your life. I'll show you how to take a real rest. Walk with me and work with me—watch how I do it. Learn the unforced rhythms of grace. I won't lay anything heavy or ill-fitting on you. Keep company with me and you'll learn to live freely and lightly."

Freely and lightly. Isn't that what we want for ourselves? And on our best days it's what we want for others too. Forgiveness frees them to pursue their own path with God and frees you to move on—on yours.[33]

---

32 Amy Lyles Wilson and Marjorie J. Thompson, "Our Resistance to Forgiveness," in *Forgiveness: Perspectives on Making Peace with Your Past* (Nashville, TN: Fresh Air Books, 2008), pp. 60–61.

33 Forgiveness is as simple as this and much more complicated than that. If you've experienced trauma, betrayal, or broken trust, forgiveness will look very different for you. This reading is not meant in any way to be an exhaustive treatment of

---

ALL THE MORE

- Hands down, Margaret Silf's method of forgiveness seeking in the Examen is my favorite. It's worth quoting in its entirety. And practicing. "Sorrow: With hindsight you may realize that much of your reaction to the events of the day has been centered on your own kingdom. This may have led you to fail to respond to the cry of another person, or to allow your own preoccupations to take center stage and crowd out other people's needs. Your day may have left little space for an awareness of God or of his creation. Whatever inadequacies you find in your day's living, let them be there before God now, not for judgment, but for his Spirit to hover over the mess, bringing wholeness out of brokenness, as once that same Spirit brought creation out of chaos. Express your sorrow to God, and confidently ask for his healing and forgiveness."[34]

---

forgiving others, but rather a reflection on the daily forgiveness we extend to other broken people like ourselves.

34 Silf, 105.

day 13: listen

*"[Jesus] calls his own sheep by name and leads them out. When he
gets them all out, he leads them and they follow because they are
familiar with his voice."*

— JOHN 10:3

One of the most common questions I'm asked as a spiritual director is, "How do I hear the voice of God?" Embedded in that question are several more:

- How will I know what to do?
- How will I be comforted when I'm sad?
- How will I know when something/someone is good or bad for me?

Many of us were raised on stories from the Scriptures where God spoke in an audible voice. Adam and Eve heard God's voice in the Garden of Eden (Genesis 3:8). Moses heard God's voice from the burning bush (Exodus 3:4–6) and Israel heard it from Mount Sinai (Exodus 20:1–22). In the New Testament, all those present at Jesus' baptism by John the Baptist heard God speak a blessing over him (Matthew 3:17). Saul and his friends both saw and heard Jesus (Acts 9:3–7).

The sheer quantity of occasions when God chose to speak audibly can make a girl feel very self-conscious about NOT hearing a loud, clear voice in response to her prayers. AND I know very few people who would admit that they carry on chat sessions—out loud—with the Almighty on a regular basis. So how exactly do people communicate with their Creator?

Here's what I've absorbed over the years about listening to God's voice. God speaks through:

- Scriptures
- People
- Tradition (hymns, creeds, spiritual texts)
- Spiritual Heart (reason, personal experience)[35]

The first half of my spiritual life I focused on the first three to the exclusion of the last one. I expected God to tell me what to do through bible verses and hymns. I sought out mentors with an earnestness that rivaled Anne of Green Gables. I just knew the right person would guide me in the way I should go. Bless me—that girl did the best she could. And I obeyed as best I could with all that I read, sang, and heard from wise women. (I was SUCH a try-hard.)

I gave very little thought to how God might be speaking in the events of my daily life. More significantly, I didn't trust in my own ability to discern for myself what God might be saying. I assumed that everyone else knew better than me about my life and my heart. (I was taught that on more than one occasion as well.)

---

35 As defined by theologian Richard Hooker in his theory of the Three-Legged Stool of Authority.

I placed all the emphasis outside of myself and did not value the internal movements of my soul.

The Examen helped bring me into balance. I didn't have to rely only on a Scripture passage or ancient prayer. I also had what happened in my own life in the last twenty-four hours to consider. Dennis Hamm, SJ explains it this way, "If we are to listen for the God who creates and sustains us, we need to take seriously and prayerfully the meeting between the creatures we are and all else that God holds lovingly in existence. That 'interface' is the felt experience of my day. It deserves prayerful attention. It is a big part of how we know and respond to God."[36]

I knew heaps ABOUT God, but I didn't KNOW God very well at this point in my life. On top of it all, I was pretty new to myself as well. The Enneagram was introducing me to my unconscious fears and desires but getting to know myself and God was a slow process for me.

Because I love a good all-or-nothing pendulum swing, in the early stages of praying the Examen, I chucked everything but personal experience out the window. I couldn't believe no one had told me about this. I was giddy at the idea that God was with me in all the things. I gradually started to feel that way too.

The feeling of nearness to God brought me back to my bedroom on Alden Street as a six-year-old little girl. I used to rearrange my bedroom furniture for fun on a Saturday. My bed, the clear focal point of my decor, enjoyed such distinctive placements as middle of the room, smack dab in front of my double window, and, my personal favorite, kitty-corner.

My singular spiritual encounter in my memory before the age of seventeen involves me kneeling at the top of my bed (kitty-cor-

---

36   Hamm, "Rummaging for God: Praying Backwards through Your Day."

ner as it happens) and "knowing" that God and I were one. That's all I've got. Me staring at the corner of my bedroom wallpapered with red and white stripes and contemplating oneness with the Divine. If I thought about it the next day or maintained any conscious awareness of this nearness, I don't remember.

Thinking about it now I am teary. From six to thirty-six, God's nearness to me was hidden from my heart by too many rules and too much knowledge. BUT like Taylor Swift sings in "Invisible String," a single thread connected me to God all through the years. The Examen opened my eyes to that precious thread of knowing and taught me how to cherish it—not above all things but along with everything else.

The more I felt as if I knew God, the more I trusted God. And the more I trusted God, the more I relied on the truth that I wouldn't be led down any wrong paths. Only then could I trust myself to hear God's voice in my ordinary life.

I realized that God works in all things that exist; therefore, our intimate thoughts, feelings, desires, fears, and our responses to the people and things around us are not just the accidental ebb and flow of our inner lives, but rather the privileged moments through which God creates and sustains a unique relationship with each of us.[37] God and I were creating our own language that featured the words, people, and activities of my very own world.

One of my mentors in spiritual direction training described the result of communication with God as creating an inner home where you feel loved. When things outside of you get crazy, you can go inside and come home. I hold onto that image of coming

---

37 "A Pocket Guide to Jesuit Education," Boston College: Division of Mission and Ministry, https://www.bc.edu/content/bc-web/offices/mission-ministry/publications/a-pocket-guide-to-jesuit-education.html.

home to love when I feel overwhelmed with the competing voices from my day.

I'm grateful for the Examen and for the love I know now as a result of practicing it. Finding your own language with God is worth the effort. And a whole lot simpler than maybe you were led to believe. So, have at it. Here's a list to get you started or jog your memory. It's a list of stuff that make up a life. It is also what God might use to communicate with you.

> **The result of communication with God is an inner home where you feel loved.**

- A penny, bird, or butterfly
- Three people saying the same things—repetition
- Imagination
- Children
- Creation/nature
- Emotions
- Pets/animals
- Music/art
- Movement/dance
- Relationships/community
- Suffering
- Metaphor/symbolism
- Words

ALL THE MORE

- Consider the difference between knowing a lot about God and knowing God. Which feels most true of you today?
- Can you identify what you rely on most for a sense of nearness to God?
- Do you trust yourself to hear God's voice? Why or why not? Many women describe being told to treat with suspicion their own thoughts and feelings. What causes you to doubt yourself?
- Would you say you and God have your own language? What specific words, images, or signs does God use to speak to you? If you don't at this moment and sense a desire rising in your soul for a deeper connection to God, express this to God now.

day 14: healing

"If we do not transform our pain,
we will most assuredly transmit it."
— Richard Rohr

A gift I give myself is a monthly appointment with my spiritual director. I welcome the careful attention of another to my life and my soul. I look forward to my time with her, and this month was no exception. The month prior had been full to overflowing with glimpses of the Divine, and I couldn't wait to share these moments with her.

I recounted my sightings to her with gratitude and wonder. I didn't want to move on from the sweet gladness that comes from giving thanks. As I looked at the candle flame between us (which represents God's presence in the room), something shifted. I knew that wasn't all I had to say. I began to speak of a discomfort—a weight—that rests right between my shoulders. I lamented this burden and wondered aloud how I could continue to bear it.

She asked me simply, "Have you invited Jesus into your discomfort?" My breath caught. I knew I hadn't. I had asked God what to do about it. I had asked for help to get out of it. I'd even cried out in anger and desperation, "How long????" The thought crossed my mind fleetingly that I knew better—that I should have asked Jesus to be with me in it—that I asked other people that very same question regarding situations in their own life.

Her face and the candle gently brought me back to the present. To the invitation to invite the wounded, scarred healer to be with me in my pain. A quote from Anne Lamott floated to the surface, "My mind is a bad neighborhood I try not to go into alone." I live by that quote. I know to get my thoughts into the gentle hands of trusted friends every day. But here I was all alone with this boulder of discomfort, and I realized the danger I was in. It is not safe for me to be alone with this weight—to carry this weight alone.

You and I are not made to carry heavy burdens on our own. Our backs break and our hearts fail. Even worse, we become hurt people who hurt people. St. Ambrose said, "No one heals himself by wounding another," but we've surely tried. When you think about the worst pain you've experienced, it's often at the hands of a wounded soul who hasn't processed their own pain.

It is wise to do an inventory of your pain on a regular basis. The Examen gives you the perfect opportunity to ask the hard questions of your soul: What pain am I holding onto? What wound still needs healing? Do I feel God near in my sorrow? Have I asked for God's presence with me? The Examen not only reveals the wounds that need healing but also the path to mending your soul.

Martin Luther King Jr., a master of describing pain, said, "As my sufferings mounted I soon realized that there were two ways in which I could respond to my situation—either to react with bitterness or seek to transform the suffering into a creative force. I decided to follow the latter course." I

It is wise to do an inventory of your pain on a regular basis.

imagine God and community aided his work of transforming his unjust pain into a powerful crusade for unity and freedom. This kind of effort needs helping hands. Do not struggle against loneliness, abandonment, betrayal, and grief alone. People who love you have the power to help mend you.

Many years ago, I asked God to show me what heals me. I knew the verse that said Jesus's wounds heal us, but how did that work? I noticed that I felt closest to God in nature—specifically within a forest of trees and by a body of water. My thoughts and feelings naturally moved toward God when I was in nature.

Wendell Berry, a fervent lover of nature, said this, "Healing is impossible in loneliness; it is the opposite of loneliness. Conviviality is healing. To be healed we must come with all the other creatures to the feast of Creation."[38] It makes sense to me that life God created—nature, people—heals the created. When my grief or sadness weigh me down, I get into the forest or by a lake with people who love me. Outdoors is big enough to absorb anything I can throw at it.

The Examen reveals what needs healing and how God specifically works in your life to heal you. The greatest gift of the Examen is the simple reminder that God is with you. God's presence heals. Daily bathing in divine love and grace soothes a soul.

Jesus promised to be with us to the end. He said it was better for him to return to heaven and send the Spirit to be with all people, in all places, at all times. Ask to see every place God fills. Invite God to sit down next to your pain and carry it for you. "So we're not giving up. How could we! Even though on the outside it often looks like things are falling apart on us, on the inside, where God is

---

38 Wendell Berry, "The Body and the Earth," in *The Art of the Commonplace: The Agrarian Essays of Wendell Berry* (Counterpoint, 2003), 98.

making new life, not a day goes by without his unfolding grace....
There's far more here than meets the eye." (2 Corinthians 4:16–18)

ALL THE MORE

Examen for Identifying Inner Wounds

- I ask God to make his presence known to me in this moment. I place my hands, palms up, in a gesture of receptivity.
- I spend a few moments in gratitude, thanking God for one or two of the blessings, big and small, that I've received today.
- I ask God to show me a wound in my heart at this moment. This wound causes me to feel hurt, frightened, angry, resentful, or remorseful. I allow God to take me to that difficult place in my soul. Courageously sit in the midst of this difficult moment. Perhaps I ask Jesus to hold my hand as I prayerfully relieve the worst parts.
- I ask God to show me the strongest emotion I have at this very moment as I rehash this painful experience. I speak aloud to God about how I'm feeling. I say, "God, I am furious (or sad, or grief-stricken, or confused)." I sit with God and with these feelings for a moment.
- I ask God to show me how this might become worse—growing in size or becoming infected. If I were to allow this wound to lead me away from faith, hope, and love, what might that look like? Concretely, in what ways might this wound tempt me to behave poorly? I ask God to help me prevent this from happening. If I need grace to help me guard against this, I ask for that grace from God right now.

- I sit in the silence for just a moment, giving God a chance to do whatever God wants with me right now. It's okay if God seems to be saying and doing nothing at all. I trust that He will heal this wound in His own time and His own way.
- I prayerfully daydream for just a moment, imagining a day when I am no longer feeling wounded about this. What would that be like? What might be my attitudes, perspectives, thoughts, feelings, words, and actions if I were truly a recovered soul? What grace would I need to begin to heal? I ask God for that grace right now.[39]

---

39 Mark E. Thibodeaux, *Reimagining the Ignatian Examen: Fresh Ways to Pray from Your Day* (Chicago, IL: Loyola Press, 2015).

day 15: solitude

"For prayer is nothing else than being on terms
of friendship with God."
— St. Teresa of Avila

Have you ever noticed how difficult it is to reach out to a friend when you are feeling pain? It seems nearly impossible to press the green phone icon and connect when what you have to say is that you feel hurt, angry, or ashamed. (There are whole books written about how shame and hurt keep us from belonging to ourselves and others.) There is an unspoken rule that says we are the most likable and enjoyable to be around when we are happy. Pain so often leads to isolation and loneliness.

I wonder if you can connect to any of these realities: A barren woman ceases to attend baby showers, then church, then friends' parties to avoid the presence of children. The newly divorced man slowly pulls away from his friend group because he is more aware of his single status in a room full of couples. One battling a chronic illness avoids phone calls and outings with loved ones because there is no good news to report, no milestone to celebrate, no end in sight to the pain. You are the most tempted to isolate when you experience pain.

Pain exacerbates the truth of the human existence: You are in this alone. No one lives for you or dies with you. At your very core, in your deepest inner life, you are alone with God. According to Henri Nouwen, you can do one of two things in your aloneness: we can cultivate a garden of solitude or experience an excruciating aloneness. The *Urban Dictionary* defines solitude as "being alone without any regrets, sadness, or depression."[40] The *Collins Dictionary* defines it this way, "The state of being alone especially when this is peaceful and pleasant."[41]

Loneliness, on the other hand, signals a lack or a loss of companionship or company. Depression and sadness accompany loneliness, and the peace of solitude is hard to find. And just as you feel lonely when you do not connect with friends or family, you feel the same toward God. Pain causes you to pull away from God too.

Prayer—beyond begging or cursing—is often the first thing to go when you suffer from chronic emotional or physical pain. Lack of communication intensifies your loneliness from God and you get stuck in a vicious cycle.

Examen opens a small window through which you can begin to see the light. It may not be the dawn rising or the light at the end of the tunnel, but it is the light of a candle that brightens up a small part of a darkened room. Examen invites you to notice anything, absolutely anything, that brought you any kind of faith, hope, or love in your day.

---

40   "Solitude," *Urban Dictionary*, https://www.urbandictionary.com/define. php?term=Solitude.

41   "Solitude Definition and Meaning," *Collins English Dictionary* (HarperCollins Publishers Ltd), https://www.collinsdictionary.com/us/dictionary/english/ solitude.

And over time, you cultivate solitude. You create a space that is reserved for God alone, to join with God in attending to your soul. You alone may carry the disease in your body or the pain in your heart, but sharing it with God can mean you carry it differently in yourself. And when you are at rest in yourself, it opens you up to companionship with your Creator.

> And when you are at rest in yourself, it opens you up to companionship with your Creator.

One of my directees writes beautifully about her loneliness caused by her daughter's illness and the transformation of it into companionship with Jesus.

I was first introduced to Examen during a very difficult season of my life. My daughter had been diagnosed with anorexia and was suffering deeply. Naturally, I was as well. My prayers on her behalf felt desperate, frantic even. Yet these impassioned pleas often seemed as though they slipped down the rabbit hole—lost or unattended to at best. I found myself feeling painfully confused and alone. While I didn't necessarily feel angry with God, I also didn't know how the two of us could continue communicating in terms that felt safe and fruitful for me.

When my spiritual director introduced me to the practice of Examen, I almost immediately sensed that within this gracious and collaborative posture, there was room to trust and to breathe. This exchange steeped in curiosity allows me to collaborate with the Creator of the Universe in ways that leaves me feeling both empowered and embraced all at once. It fosters an environment in which God and I can take a look at my day in a manner of togetherness. I have started to see His

compassionate spirit in my life and the lives of those I love in
new and specific terms. It has helped tame the anxious energy
I tend to bring to my prayer life. In exchange, with time and
practice, it is allowing me to grow in my ability to walk out
our present narrative with a greater sense of His peace, pres-
ence, and deep care for us all.

Nothing changed for her as it relates to her daughter. She still
suffers the daily pain of watching her daughter struggle toward
health. She still works tirelessly with the team of doctors and care-
givers to give her daughter the best shot at recovery.

The difference is that, through examining her daily moments,
she now sees God present in her narrative. She is learning to engage God in her solitude and is closer to feeling peaceful than
before. Nouwen says it better, "What is new is that we no longer experience the many things, people, and events as causes for
worry, but begin to experience them as the rich variety of ways in
which God makes His presence known to us."[42]

My last thought on this is that when lonely people seek relationship with other lonely people, it doesn't usually work out
well. The work in between loneliness and community is solitude.
Until you learn to rest easy with yourself, you will struggle to form
healthy attachments to others. You will look to others to fulfill
companionship needs that only God can. Solitude causes "our
hearts [to] become like quiet cells where God can dwell, wherever
we go and whatever we do."[43] And hearts at rest can join together
and listen to the music of God together.

---

42   Henri Nouwen, *Making All Things New and Other Classics* (Grand Rapids, MI:
     Zondervan, 2000), 24.
43   Nouwen, 33.

ALL THE MORE

- When have you experienced a season of loneliness? Do you remember what brought you back to God, yourself, and community?
- Brené Brown says that shame needs three things to grow: secrecy, silence, and judgment. Can you identify a safe person who can hear from you when you aren't doing well? Reach out to that person as an act of kindness toward yourself and you will stunt the growth of shame in your life.
- Nouwen further describes solitude as enabling "us to live active lives in the world, while remaining always in the presence of God." Check in with yourself today with the Examen. See if you can identify the presence of God in your otherwise hectic day.

day 16: notice

*"Tell me what you pay attention to and
I will tell you who you are."*
— José Ortega y Gasset

On a scale of 1 to 10, how observant are you of your surroundings? Do you notice when a friend gets a haircut or if someone rearranges the furniture or paints a new color in the living room? Do you pick up on the moods of the people around you? Are you cognizant of the weather and if you feel hot or cold? Do your eyes clock who comes and goes in a crowded room or who sits by whom at the dinner party?

When you think about it, it's difficult to notice anything specific given the plethora of information that comes at us in a day. Most of us have to work hard to pay attention to the things that are important to us. I no longer rely on my brain and instead employ copious lists, alarms, and reminders to focus on the details that need my attention.

Overstimulation is only half the battle. You are hardwired to be a bit myopic in what you observe. The Enneagram helps us understand why. Enneagram wisdom teaches that each of us has a particular aspect of daily life we focus on above all else. Sadly, none of you will receive the "Attention to Detail" award for these fixations as they stem from the twisty nature of your personality rather than your soul. All your preoccupations earn you is a lifetime of working to overcome them.

If the Enneagram is new to you, the list of what people obsess over won't be. You can still find yourself in the descriptions even if the numbers still make no sense to you.

Focus of Attention Based on Enneagram Personality Type

- **Ones:** Errors, mistakes, and problems that need fixing—so you can fix it and quiet your inner critic
- **Twos:** Other people's needs—so you can meet those needs and earn the approval and affirmation you long to hear
- **Threes:** Accomplishment of tasks and goals—so you can gain recognition, approval, and admiration from others
- **Fours:** What is missing—so you can continue longing for it
- **Fives:** Detachment and observation—so you can maintain boundaries and ensure you will not be catastrophically depleted
- **Sixes:** Hyper-vigilance to predict and plan for worst-case scenarios—so you can prevent potential harm
- **Sevens:** Best-case thinking—so you can engage in exciting stimulation and avoid anything that brings you discomfort
- **Eights:** Control—so you can protect yourself and others from being controlled or harmed
- **Nines:** Other people's agendas—so you know how to keep the peace

As an Enneagram One, I notice my obsession with spotting mistakes or problems the most when I've been gone from my house for the day or the weekend. Bless the hearts of the three males I live with when I arrive home. I see first any dishes or cups left on the coffee table in the living room and head straight for them. As I'm carrying those to the sink, I'm surveying all surfaces for paperwork, packages, JUNK—anything that doesn't belong.

As I clear and place objects in their right places, I'm asking my family if they've done what they said they were going to do while I was away. I've emptied the trash before they answer and begin dusting as they finish their welcome backs. I barely register that I'm doing any of it until one of them mocks me for it. I don't blame them—I feel worn out just reading back that paragraph!

More exhausting is when I'm not conscious of how I notice all the problems that need fixing in me and rain down judgment and criticism to motivate myself to change. I'm not nearly as focused on this as I used to be, but my ways have become more subtle and harder to detect.

What drew me to the Examen was the hope of seeing something else. Something other than what was wrong and what I needed to do to fix it. I longed to see God—to see how Jesus was making all things new as he promised.

The Examen roots itself in the core belief that God is present in the world and in the lives of all human beings. I like the way Barbara Brown Taylor puts it, "Earth is so thick with divine possibility that it is a wonder we can walk anywhere without cracking our shins on altars."[44] I wanted to stop looking where I was going and bump into God on my path.

---

44 Barbara Brown Taylor, *An Altar in the World: A Geography of Faith* (New York: HarperOne, 2010), 15.

It's a steep learning curve to retrain your mind and heart to see God instead of what you're used to seeing. Our default settings make it so. The world is crowded with God BUT we have to make the choice whether or not to look for the evidence.

I think about my phone's GPS and how boggled it gets when I stop for gas on a long trip. Maps is zeroed in on my final destination and scrambles to give me new paths to get there. It will keep rerouting until I change the location of where I'm headed.

The gift of the Examen is that it gives you the opportunity to look for God every twenty-four hours. "God is always inviting us to encounter the transcendent in the everyday. The key is noticing. This insight—that finding God is about noticing—helps the seeker in two ways. First, it makes the quest straightforward [contemplates real events vs. abstract concepts]....Second, noticing helps you realize that your life is already suffused with the presence of God. Once you begin to look around and allow yourself to take a chance to believe in God, you will easily see God at work in your life."[45]

---

45   Martin, *The Jesuit Guide to (Almost) Everything: A Spirituality for Real Life*, 111–112.

ALL THE MORE

- What do you notice on a regular basis?
- What distracts you from noticing God?
- How does believing that God will show up change your approach to prayer? If that's hard for you to believe, can you come to prayer as if you believe God is present? Try it. You can't mess up, remember?

day 17: simplicity

*"The ability to simplify means to eliminate the unnecessary
so that the necessary may speak."*
— HANS HOFMANN

I like a clean sight line. By that I mean I like the surfaces in my home to be free of clutter. I don't have a lot of knickknacks because too much stuff creates chaos in my brain. Clutter might go unnoticed if all is well in my world, but when something is off (much of the time)—watch out countertop! Steer clear pile on the table! I can walk into a room and spot the thing that doesn't belong with dizzying speed. It will be put away, thrown away, or shoved out of sight faster than my family can ask, "Hey, did you see my (fill in the blank)?"

I won't soon live down the computer chip, tool, paper, etc. that I've thrown away in the name of a clean sight line. I contend that I'm simply obedient to the ethos of nineteenth century British designers like William Morris who famously said, "Have nothing in your houses that you do not know to be useful or believe to be beautiful." (Who could argue with that?)

In her book *The Next Right Thing*, Emily P. Freeman coins the phrase "soul minimalist." She builds on the ideas of Joshua Becker in his *Becoming Minimalist* podcast and book. Becker says that minimalism is not that you should own nothing. But that nothing should own you. He points out that you have regular, seasonal input of stuff in your homes that comes by way of gifts, papers, bills, decorations for seasonal celebrations, and clothing. If you don't have a practice of decluttering or throwing used/unnecessary items away, your home becomes filled with things you don't need or want.

Freeman argues that our souls can be the same way. Your soul receives frequent input but lacks regular output. Think about all that you process in a day—the weird phone call you keep replaying, the too short (or too long!) hug someone gave you, the song that reminded you of a painful memory, the comment that stings, etc. You are taking things into your soul all the time.

I'm so drawn to the phrase "soul minimalist" because I battle mental clutter every day. Reading the news (I gave up watching years ago) is enough to send me over the edge regularly. The facts themselves cause distress, and the way facts or distortions of facts are presented generate even more anxiety. (My daily habit is to read news from multiple outlets with various biases. I read coverage and opinions from people who don't look like me or think like me. My hope is to find some kernel of truth in the distillation of all that I read.)

News is soul-cluttering enough. Facebook and Instagram can be soul-crushing. No one ever finished scrolling and thought, "Gosh, I feel so grounded and peaceful. I feel so loved." Twitter, though, is the worst. If you want to watch people name call and argue for the sake of it, spend a little time on Twitter. I hold firm boundaries around my social media use (I will never be accused of being easy-breezy), and I still notice at night that I'm thinking about something I read earlier in the day. Or I'm worrying that a close friend and I believe very different things about an important issue.

Even worse, news and social media provide only a fraction of what crowds my soul as I lay my head down to sleep. I hold onto a frustrating exchange with my son and worry that the apathy displayed in our conversation will mean he won't be gainfully employed when he's forty. I do the math on what's due before the next paycheck over and over (I'm terrible at math and have been known to make HUGE mistakes when adding up what's due). When I'm really avoiding the hard stuff of fractured relationships or a friend's cancer diagnosis, I panic about whether or not they will continue to make my favorite scented candle or hair product.

I also like to move. I take long daily walks, bustle about my house, and prefer standing to sitting. But I've learned after many sleepless nights and constant worry that I wouldn't make it through my days without a little stillness. Between the mental clutter and the physical busyness, I'm desperate for some grounding and centering. Freeman writes, "Stillness is to the soul as decluttering is to a home. Silence and stillness allow you to sift through your day. The silence serves as a colander helping you decide what to hold onto and allowing what you don't need to gently fall through, making space to access creativity and courage, quieting to hear the voice of God."[46]

The Examen offers a way to practice the regular output of what you don't need or want each day. As you invite God into the daily experiences, feelings, and thoughts of your life, you choose what to savor or keep and what to let go of. You ask for grace and

---

46   Emily P. Freeman, *The Next Right Thing: A Simple, Soulful Practice for Making Life Decisions* (Grand Rapids, MI: Revell, 2019).

help for the things that seem to own you. You acknowledge what drew you to love and what drove you to fear. Within the Examen, you cultivate a loving space to say what you need to say, ask for the help you need, and seek repair in your relationships with God, self, and others.

Becoming a soul minimalist means "clearing clutter and creating space for silence, letting your soul know it's safe to come out, and making room to listen."[47] It is work to make space for silence. Nobody will hand it to you. You will have to make many intentional choices to give your soul the room it needs to breathe. Those who know me well can tell when I haven't made those choices. I can tell. I'm loving myself, God, and others well when I sit on my daybed and place my soul in God's loving embrace.

> The Examen offers a way to practice the regular output of what you don't need or want each day.

---

47 Freeman, *The Next Right Thing: A Simple, Soulful Practice for Making Life Decisions.*

ALL THE MORE

- Imagine the Examen as a daily decluttering of your mind and soul. Pay particular attention to what idea, feeling, or thought seems to own you.
- Practice letting go of what robs your soul of love, faith, and hope.
- Consider creating boundaries around what you take in each day. That might involve limiting your exposure to certain people or things (that judgy friend, the news, social media, the kind of books you read or the TV shows you watch). Notice what causes you to feel more loving at the end of the day and what causes you to feel more fearful. Show yourself compassion by saying no or that's enough to the life-draining things in your life.

day 18: rest

*"Almost everything will work again if you unplug it
for a few minutes, including you."*
— ANNE LAMOTT

My lower back bothers me (to say nothing of my feet, hips, and knees!) and my chiropractor wondered aloud about my bed mattress. I told him it was a ten-year-old pillow-top mattress. The look on his face told me I needed something different! I researched online the best mattresses for side sleepers with back problems. I read hundreds of reviews and compared the top-rated choices. I narrowed the list down to my favorite and then stopped short when I had to give my credit card info. Was I really going to spend this kind of money on a mattress?

I left the screen open and wandered outside to see if any of my neighbors and friends were out and about (walking outside clears my head and helps me avoid unpleasant tasks). I started polling my friends on the importance of their mattresses. Everyone said some version of, "You spend one-third of your life on it! Spend the money!" When I asked them when they had last "spent the money" on a new mattress, I got a shocking number of excuses.

You know sleep is important. You know that most people need seven to eight hours of sleep to rejuvenate and rest. So where is this resistance to creating an optimal environment that allows you to rest coming from? I think the reasons are as varied as the number of people who respond to the question. One of the ones that comes up often is the frustration with being a human who has limitations. The need for sleep, food, and bathroom breaks feels like a "wart in the a** of progress" (my dad's colorful phrase) and feels needy and unhelpful on top of that.

Jesus showed us a better way. Rest and renewal are woven into the very fabric of who God is. (And last time I checked, humans are made in the image of God.) For example, God took a break on the seventh day of creating the world, blessed the day and called it holy (Genesis 2:2). God also gave us a day of the week to rest and remember all that had been done for us (Exodus 34:21). God even asked the people to give the land a rest from producing a crop every seven years (Exodus 23:11). Rhythms of rest provide the backdrop to much of the biblical narrative of God's people.

And Jesus loved a good rest. He liked to get away on his own to renew his energy after hard work (Mark 6). He sat down by wells after long walks (John 4:6). He even slept on a boat during a storm he was so tired (Mark 4). Isn't it interesting that he chose to need food and sleep? Jesus attached no shame to his physical needs. Why do you?

One of my favorite verses is Psalm 103:14 (NIV) "For [God] knows how we are formed, he remembers that we are dust. The Message says that God, "...keeps in mind that we're made of mud." You aren't fooling anyone—including God. You need rest. It's only human.

So, let's say you've cleared the hurdle of knowing that you need rest. Let's further rule out any physical pain or discomfort because you showed kindness to yourself and bought the good mattress. So many struggle to fall asleep at night or wake in the middle of the night and struggle to fall back to sleep. What keeps you awake?

I worry often that some things will never change. Mind you, I do not like change when I do not like it. But when something is hard, I worry it will always be hard. And I wish it would change. The fear that something painful will not change is what keeps me up at night.

Sleeping with Bread is hands down the most delightful book written about the Examen. Matthew Linn, a Jesuit priest, along with his brother, Dennis, and sister-in-law, Sheila, created this easy to read picture book to bring the Examen to life.

The story that opens the book is about bread. "During the bombing raids of WWII, thousands of children were orphaned and left to starve. The fortunate ones were rescued and placed in refugee camps where they received food and good care. But many of these children could not sleep at night, fearing waking up to find themselves once again homeless and without food. Finally, someone hit upon the idea of giving each child a piece of bread to hold at bedtime. Holding the bread, these children could finally sleep in peace. All through the night the bread reminded them, 'today I ate and I will eat again tomorrow.'"[48]

Can you relate to those scared children? Worries, fears, anger, and hurts crowd your thoughts and push sleep away. The belief that there won't be enough for tomorrow—time, money, energy, endurance, love—looms large. The floating anxiety that you are missing something important in your relationship with God or

---

48   Dennis Linn, Sheila Fabricant Linn, and Matthew Linn, *Sleeping with Bread: Holding What Gives You Life* (Mahwah: Paulist Press, 1995), 1.

loved ones grabs hold of your heart and keeps your body and mind from rest.

The Examen is a daily method to bring forward the ways in which God shows up to you. A way to see all that God provides for you on a regular basis. When you take the time to place yourself in God's presence and review the events of the last twenty-four hours, you offer your heart, soul, mind, and body the possibility of nourishment and rest.

By practicing the Examen, you learn to receive the gifts of your days as daily bread. And like these children, you can benefit from holding your "daily bread" while you sleep. The insights of a few minutes' reflection can nourish you and help strengthen you for the next day and all the days ahead.

> By practicing the Examen, you learn to receive the gifts of your days as daily bread.

I'm now in the habit of noticing nature when I walk or sit outside. I take note of the colors, animals, and trees that populate the outdoors. What I see and enjoy in natures frequently comes up in my Examen. When I'm tempted to believe (at 3 a.m. no doubt) that nothing will ever change, God reminds me of the trees—how their leaves change—and the birds—how their nests change locations.

I hold on to these realities and allow them to calm me. Rest comes more easily when I'm regularly in touch with the One who alone is able to make all things new. And evidence from my Examen comforts me in ways that simply "knowing" that God is able does not.

ALL THE MORE

- Can you identify in yourself any resistance to rest or human limitations? Tell God about it.
- What keeps you up at night? Ask God to show you how He is present to you in that situation or fear.
- What can you hold onto tonight as you fall asleep? Where did you see faith, hope, or love today? Allow it to comfort your soul as you lay down to rest your body.

day 19: generosity

> *"It is rare indeed that people give. Most people guard and keep;*
> *they suppose that it is they themselves and what they identify with*
> *themselves that they are guarding and keeping, whereas what they*
> *are actually guarding and keeping is their system of reality and*
> *what they assume themselves to be."*
> –JAMES BALDWIN, *THE FIRE NEXT TIME*

I am the grateful daughter of two incredibly generous parents. They are openhanded with their time, praise, resources, and laughter. They are ridiculously generous with their grandkids. My lived experience is that I have always had what I need (and more), and I have never worried about not having enough. I live with the reality of a safety net, and it is no small privilege.

My story, and my idealistic and positive demeanor, set me up well to assume the best about other people—and I do. And yet, it came as a surprise to me that I didn't give God the same indulgence. When I wrote in my journal that first week of the Spiritual Exercises about generosity—being willing to receive all that God has for me—I didn't know how much wider my arms would have to stretch to take in all that God was giving.

A lesser known pearl of Ignatian wisdom is something called the "plus sign." Jesuits will often refer to it as "putting the plus sign on it" or "plus sign others." To "plus sign" someone is to give them the benefit of the doubt—to assume the best interpretation of another's actions toward you. The Ignatian plus sign, also called the presupposition, comes from the Spiritual Exercises. Here is a modern translation of Ignatius's words:

> For a good relationship to develop …a mutual respect is very necessary. …Every good Christian adopts a more positive acceptance of someone's statement rather than a rejection of it out of hand. And so a favorable interpretation …should always be given to the other's statement, and confusions should be cleared up with Christian understanding.[49]

Embedded in this ancient teaching to look for the best in others is the assumption that you aren't very good at it. If you were, you wouldn't need a reminder. Humans assign meaning to every look, word, action, and body movement that comes our way. It is not a far leap for most of us to decide that another's actions intend us harm.

How many arguments have ended with you or the other person saying, "That's not what I meant!"? The fight is now about intent versus impact. Your sister didn't mean to hurt your feelings by sharing that story, but the impact of her telling it is hurt and broken trust.

---

49   David L. Fleming, SJ, *Draw Me Into Your Friendship* (Saint Louis, MO: Institute of Jesuit Sources, 1996).

Plus sign asks you to back up to the moment before someone begins to speak and—right there—make the decision to accept the best possible version of whatever you are about to hear. Plus sign puts the burden of responsibility on the hearer to supply the most generous interpretation, not the speaker to defend the intention of the words. More than that, if you do hear criticism, judgment, or insensitivity in another's words, it is on you to ask for clarification of their meaning. You don't walk away from a conversation wondering about their intent—you stay until you understand fully what is being said. The hope is that by being clear, you can be kind—or at least pursue a path of kindness. "Clear is kind. Unclear is unkind."[50]

Putting the plus sign on it takes work and courage—and wisdom and discernment. Most people deserve your generosity—some don't. (A good way to tell if you are talking to a regular flawed human or someone who doesn't deserve your trust right now is to go through Brené Brown's BRAVING inventory.[51] And wouldn't you know it, her definition of generosity could have been pulled straight from Ignatius' journal, "Generosity: You extend the most generous interpretation possible to the intentions, words, and actions of others.")[52]

The reason this matters to you when praying the Examen is that God often speaks to you through the people in your life. Through the ordinary actions and words that come to you by other people God made. And if you lack generosity in your evaluation of other's interactions with you, you just might assume God means you harm too.

---

50 Brené Brown, *Dare to Lead* (Random House, 2018), 48.
51 For the full BRAVING Inventory, go to https://daretolead.brenebrown.com/ and see Downloads.
52 Brown, *Dare to Lead*, 226.

For example, during the "review your day" portion of the Examen, let's say you recall the strange look you got from someone at church, the lack of response from your best friend to your text, and the frustration in your boss's voice in her comments to you. Without the plus sign, your day is full of people who were unkind to you. It would make sense, with that kind of evidence, to conclude that God isn't very kind either.

But what if you plus signed the people of your day. What if you assumed that the person at church was preoccupied and not looking at you at all, what if you trust that your best friend will respond when he can, what if you choose to cut your boss some slack given the stressful season she is experiencing. All of a sudden the day takes on a different feel—and so does how you see God.

One of the questions I ask those who come for spiritual direction is, "How do you see God?" To probe a little further, I ask for three to five words that remind them of God. So many of the words used to describe God have something to do with another broken relationship in their lives—and nothing to do with God's character.

You do this too. So do I. Because you don't see God, you look at the next best thing—what God has made—and make some quick judgments. What if instead you chose to extend the most generous interpretation possible to the intentions, words, and actions of God? What if you decided that everything Jesus said about God is true? What if you gave God a fraction of the generosity that God gives you? I think it could help. I think you might see things you didn't before.

ALL THE MORE

- God often speaks to us through the people in our lives. How can we humbly and generously interpret others' words so we do not miss out on gifts from God?
- List the words or names that best reflect your image of God. Ask for whatever you need from God as you contemplate the list—grace, healing, hope, or love.
- Think of a recent situation where you assumed the worst of another's words or actions. Would anything have changed if you put the plus sign on it?
- Meditate on John 1:1–18. Read it in the Message translation if you have it—or look it up online. Ask for the grace to plus sign your image of God.

day 20: centers

"It is a narrow mind which cannot look at a subject
from various points of view."
— George Eliot, *Middlemarch*

Neurobiological research shows that humans (and all mammals) possess three centers of intelligence—three different ways we take in and process information. Your ability to "read" your environment is helped by your head (thinking), your heart (feeling), and your gut (doing). We need all three centers to process our world fully.

Enneagram wisdom builds on what we know from science and suggests that each of us has a preferred way of interacting with the world. Our trust in our preferred center is unconscious and deep, and seeing anything from another perspective requires work.

The reason it's so hard is that we also undervalue or dismiss one of the centers because it does not help us get what we want. Welcoming or elevating the ignored center is considered by many Enneagram teachers to be the key to significant spiritual growth because it leads the way in the integration of all three.

Here's what the three centers look like:

1. The **Thinking (Head) Center** is used for gathering and sorting information, making plans, and analyzing. The eye is the sense organ associated with the thinking center. When walking into an unknown situation, a thinking question might be "How does this all fit together?" or "What's my exit strategy if this goes south?"

2. The **Feeling (Heart) Center** is used for acknowledging feelings (ours and others) and being aware of needs and agendas (ours and others). Touch and taste are the senses correlated with the feeling center. A feeling question for an unknown situation might be, "Will you like me?" or "Who are my people?" or "Where do I fit?"

3. The **Doing/Instinctive (Gut) Center** is used for accomplishing, seeking stability, and discerning power and control dynamics of an environment. The pronounced sense organs for the doing center are the ear and the nose. When walking into an unknown situation, a doing response might be, "Here I am. Deal with me." or "I don't like the way he's talking to her. He's a bad dude."[53]

When you read the center descriptions, do you connect with one over the others? If you are still having trouble finding yourself in the centers, ask yourself some questions. Do you trust reason and brain power most? Is your head knowledge what you use to get what you want and avoid what you fear? If so, you might prefer the head/thinking center.

---

53   Credit to Vanessa Sadler, Abide Enneagram Coach; Beth McCord, Your Enneagram Coach; Suzanne Stabile, Life in the Trinity.

Do you trust your relationships and feelings above everything else? Do you use your heart intuitions to get what you want and avoid what you fear? You might prefer your heart/feeling center.

Do you react instinctively and know without thinking what you like/don't like or what is good/bad? Do you rely on your gut instincts to get what you want and avoid what you fear? You might prefer your gut/doing center. Now flip it around, read the descriptions again, and consider which one you use the least.

Enneagram teachers Kathleen Hurley and Theodorre Donson describe the relationship between the centers like this, "The interconnecting relationship intended for the three centers can be pictured as a small musical ensemble....One center plays too loud and too long, disrupting the harmony of our lives. One of the other two centers takes its cue from the lead player and learns to follow even the most subtle variation on the theme of our life. Our final player, however, the third center of intelligence is ignored. It can become disgruntled and abandon us. Because it's purpose is unfamiliar to us it appears useless and unimportant." When you imagine your three centers as a musical trio, the loss of one instrument takes on a whole new meaning. You can begin to imagine what you are missing out on by not hearing the music from the quietest notes.

As a One on the Enneagram, I lead with my gut. I'm a doer. When I see a problem, I immediately act to fix it. I feel very strongly about fixing it (egged along by fear, shame, etc.) and my feelings propel my doing. I can be midway through solving a problem before asking myself, "Is this mine to do?" "Did anyone ask me to help?" "Do I even know how to fix this?"

I never even thought it through before doing something. For me, when I evaluate my thinking, it changes what I do. So, I've learned to ask questions before I jump into action. I spent years missing the crucial insights my thinking center longed to contribute to my internal conversations. My doing center exhausts me with constant movement. My thinking center offers me the opportunity to rest.

If I haven't lost you already, you may be wondering how this relates to prayer. I'm getting there. In addition to being a spiritual director, I'm also an Enneagram coach. I've worked with this personality mapping system for sixteen years, and while I won't go into all of the various layers and intricacies of it with you, the Enneagram has profoundly shaped my own spiritual journey.

Nothing else has given me more insight into my relationships with myself, God, and others. If you dislike the Enneagram or resist the idea that you fit into a box, I get it. You don't have to know or like the Enneagram for this next part to make a difference in your life. I think it helps, but you are free to take it or leave it. Okay, disclaimer given, let's move on.

Over the years, I've learned to use the Examen to see how I'm using or not using my three centers of intelligence. You can too. The Examen intentionally calls you to awareness of how God's Spirit moves in and through your heart, mind, and gut. Paying attention to what your heart feels, your mind thinks, and your body senses is critical to understanding how you exist in the world and to making changes and choices that are consistent with who you want to be.[54]

You also need all of the information your being takes in through your mind, heart, and gut to get the full picture of what God is doing in your life. "You often first experience consolations and desolations in your gut or heart. The neurons in your body

---

54   For a chart of the Preferred/Support/Repressed Centers of each Enneagram type, please see the Appendix.

and heart start sending information to your brain. You may recognize this information as cold sweats, hot flashes, hair-raising fear, a lump in your throat, clenched fists or jaw, tears, a stiff neck, heart break, heart joy, a queasy gut, headaches, elation, or illness with no preceding cause. These body and heart signals can be God's way of starting a conversation beneath the surface of your tasks and transactions to what is really affecting and guiding your life. What fears and blocks do the desolations reveal? What joys, desires, and aptitudes do the consolations reveal? Let the cues of consolation and desolation in your body and heart bring you to divine wisdom."[55]

God is a God of abundance, not scarcity. We were created to hear the whole song—with clarity and precision. Ask God to give you ears that hear it all and trust that you don't have to miss another beat.

---

55 Adele and Doug Calhoun and Clare and Scott Loughrige, *Spiritual Rhythms for the Enneagram: A Handbook for Harmony and Transformation* (IVP Books; 2019), 215.

ALL THE MORE

Examen with a Focus on Heart, Head, and Gut

- Ask to be with God as God is with you.
- Gently name a desolation, a place you feel the absence of your true self, the absence of God, or the absence of God's pleasure. Take time to notice where your heart, head, or body constrict. (**Heart** constriction may feel like your heart breaking or aching over a broken connection with others or self. **Head** constriction may present as repetitive thoughts or analysis paralysis. **Body** constriction may be experienced as tight muscles, flushed face, or sweaty palms.)
- Confess without judgment: "Today I fell into my false self when I (fill in the blank). Forgive me and make me new."
- Gently name a consolation, a place you feel the presence of God and your true self. What are you grateful for? What do you love the most? Receive and enjoy your consolations. Where do you sense God's pleasure? Where did your guidance and wisdom come from today—your heart, head, or body intelligence? Thank God for the moments when you chose to listen to your heart, head, or body.
- Pray: "Today I found life, light, and joy in (fill in the blank). Ground me in gratitude."[56]

---

56 A. Calhoun, D. Calhoun, C. Loughrige, S. Loughrige, *Spiritual Rhythms for the Enneagram: A Handbook for Harmony and Transformation*, 206–207.

day 21: values

*"The things that matter most must never be at the mercy
of the things that matter least."*
— JOHANN WOLFGANG VON GOETHE

I talk about self-care a lot as a spiritual director and Enneagram coach. My program of self-care, Nourishing Your Whole Being, highlights these truths: You are worthy of self-care; God not only encourages self-care but models it for us in Jesus; and self-care is the spiritual practice by which you remove barriers to receiving God's love.

The first stop on any self-care journey is looking at your mental landscape—the thoughts that constantly run through your head. What you think about, value, and believe impacts your ability to care for yourself. The goal is to help you create a nourishing mental environment. You get there by paying attention to your conscious and unconscious thoughts and making choices based on what you find.

One of the questions I ask in the self-care program is, "What are a few ideas, morals, values, or truths that guide your daily actions?" During a coaching session, one woman responded to my question with her own—she wanted to know how you even figure out what you value. It occurred to me that I knew in a vague sense what I valued, but I had never gone through a formal process to identify my own guiding principles. The inability to clearly state my truth knocked me off balance. I confessed to her and to myself that I had some work to do.

As it happened, Brené Brown's new book, *Dare to Lead*, was sitting on my coffee table waiting to be read. I remembered that there was a section in the book on values because I heard it in a podcast with Brené the previous week. I dove in ready to make my list.

She provides a list of over 100 values and asks the reader to narrow it down to two. She has good reasons for this and I'm inclined to believe her, but I was having the worst time doing it. In the end, I identified seven (gasp!) values or ideas that create my mental landscape. I can't tell you how bad I feel disobeying Brené. I don't do it lightly. She is a fellow Enneagram One, and I know how serious she is about her work. She wouldn't have told me to pick only two if she didn't mean it. And, likewise, I wouldn't have stuck with seven if I didn't feel equally strong about it. (I hope we can still be friends.)

What I wholeheartedly agree with is her conclusion that what you value and hold onto gets you through the hard things. Brené writes, "More often than not, our values are what lead us to the arena door—we're willing to do something uncomfortable and daring because of our beliefs. And when we get in there and stumble or fall, we need our values to remind us why we went in, especially when we are facedown, covered in dust and sweat and blood."[57]

---

57 Brown, *Dare to Lead*, 186.

I took a long look at what actually keeps me sane and buoys me when I need it most. I resisted the urge to simply copy her or someone else's list. I wrestled through my fear that I wasn't doing it right and came up with these seven ideas or words.

Katie's Values (word for word what hangs next to my bathroom mirror right now):

1. **Gratitude**—to God, others, and myself.
2. **Compassion**—toward others and myself.
3. **Generosity**—toward myself, God, and others. We are all doing the best we can and God's work in my life is for good.
4. **Abundance**—there is enough for me and everyone around me.
5. **Growth**—change is a part of life and I am capable of it.
6. **Process**—things take time.
7. **Love loop**—God is infinitely offering me love, and I have enough to give in every situation I find myself in.

What I realized as I chose my list is that all the values began as themes in prayer. When I would review my day in the Examen, certain things kept cropping up—say impatience with myself for not changing fast enough. Or frustration that I had to keep learning the same lesson over and over. I noticed that my self-talk got ugly when I didn't see the transformation I wanted in the timing I expected. I would ask God for help and a new way to think about change. *Growth* and *Process* came out of those conversations with God.

Once I had my list, I taped it to the wall in the bathroom and looked at it every morning and night. I wanted to see in black and white my values each day because I wanted to actually live by them. "Living into our values means that we do more than profess our values, we practice them. We walk our talk—we are clear about what we believe and hold important, and we take care that our intentions, words, thoughts, and behaviors align with those beliefs."[58]

Recently, a friend asked to talk with me, and she shared something that was hard for me to hear. Her observations were difficult to absorb AND I also had a nagging sense that she wasn't being completely honest with me. In the middle of the night, what she said got all twisted up inside of me as I doubted her intentions. I couldn't separate what she said (which was fair by the way) from the gut instinct that I wasn't getting the whole story. I woke up to the word *generosity* hanging on the wall and remembered another Brené definition (I really do listen to what she tells me): "Generosity: You extend the most generous interpretation possible to the intentions, words, and actions of others."[59]

I took a deep breath and asked God for help. Mercifully, I remembered moments when I was sure of my friend's love and support. I considered her circumstances and wondered where she might be coming from. I chose to assume she meant me well.

I asked if we could have a follow-up conversation two days later (I practiced *Process*—I gave myself some time). I was scared to tell her how I felt and unsure of her response but held onto the generous idea that we love each other and don't want to hurt one another.

We said what we needed to say. I told her that I thought she had more to tell me. She confirmed my instincts and apologized for not being straightforward in what she shared. We got to the heart of the matter, and in doing so, we affirmed our commitment

---

58 Brown, *Dare to Lead*, 186.
59 Brown, *Dare to Lead*, 226.

to each other as friends—not without tears but also without any regrets. Generosity 1: Friendship Yuck 0.

Without an awareness of my values, I believe our conversation would have gone differently. In this case, the Examen not only helped me identify my values but provided space for me to notice and be honest about my reactions to our conversation.

What is on your list? Talk to God about it today.

ALL THE MORE

- As you pray through your days, notice the themes. Notice where you ask for help. What do you want help to do? Who you want to be and how you want to act are clues about what you value.
- Who are you drawn to? What characteristics do you see in their life that you want?
- Print out a list of values and circle the ones that seem to stick. Pray over them. Notice if they crop up in your Examen over days and months.

day 22: location

"When you've been lost as I have," he once said, "you get good at finding your way home."
— EMILY HENRY, *A MILLION JUNES*

Owning my reality (my actual experiences, feelings, and thoughts) is hard for me. I struggle to be where I *am* because I'm tempted to live in some version of where I'm supposed to be—or where I want to be. I should be a faithful member of this denomination—so I deny my doubts about some of the teachings. I should know everything about parenting by now—so I won't admit that I still have a lot to learn. (The most relatable acronym for shame for me is "should have already mastered everything.") I should be over that offense—so I ignore the anger and hurt that simmer under the surface.

I often want to be someplace else rather than where I am. My focus on where I want to be (or think I should be), at the expense of my reality, keeps me from the awareness of God's presence in my actual life. Another way to put it is that I get lost. And it keeps me from seeing that God can and will lead me home from anywhere.

My first spiritual director, Renee, tells this story about getting lost: "Several summers ago, I was kayaking out on the largest lake in Wisconsin. For some reason, instead of paddling along the shoreline as I had done previously, I headed straight out to the center of the lake. I thought maybe I could make it all the way across. As I made my way, the wind kicked up, the waves got wavier, it began to rain, and I had no idea where I was. I scrapped my plan to reach the other side, making my destination instead the retreat center where I had put in an hour prior. After a bit of panic, I pulled out my phone, careful not to fumble and lose it to the depths of Lake Winnebago. I implored Maps, hoping to see my radiating Blue Dot. There it was, there I was, much farther out and farther east than I had imagined. Trusting that Blue Dot, I was able to get oriented and confidently head northwest toward the not yet visible red roofs of the retreat house."

When Renee opted to discover where she actually was versus where she had wanted to go, she found her way home. The storm probably helped. We humans need prompting to accept our reality sometimes.

I'm challenged by these words from the Big Book of Alcoholics Anonymous: "And acceptance is the answer to *all* my problems today. When I am disturbed, it is because I find some person, place, thing, or situation—some fact of my life—unacceptable to me, and I can find no serenity until I accept that person, place, thing, or situation as being exactly the way it is supposed to be at this moment. Nothing, absolutely nothing, happens in God's world by mistake. Until I could accept my alcoholism, I could not stay sober; unless I accept life completely on life's terms, I cannot be happy. I need to concentrate not so much on what needs to be changed in the world as on what needs to be changed in me and in my attitudes."[60]

While not an alcoholic, I can be extremely judgmental (toward myself and others), and I've never found my way to kindness and compassion without first accepting the fact of my judgmental nature. And for me, the surest way to identify my current location is to practice the Examen. When I lay out my thoughts, feelings, and actions from the last day, my reality becomes clear.

Here are some additional Examen questions I use to determine where I am:

For what moment today am I most grateful?
For what moment today am I least grateful?

When did I give and receive the most love today?
When did I give and receive the least love today?

When was I at my most loving today?
When was I at my least loving today?

When did I feel most alive today?
When did I most feel the life draining out of me?

When today did I have the greatest sense of belonging to myself, others, and God?
When did I have the least sense of belonging?

When was I happiest today?

---

60   *The Big Book of Alcoholics Anonymous* (United States: Alcoholics Anonymous, 2011), 417.

When was I saddest?

What was today's high point?
What was today's low point?

What did you feel good about today?
What was your biggest struggle today, or when did you feel sad, helpless or angry?[61]

Once you know where you are, you have the choice to accept it or engage in complicated contorting to avoid it. I wish I knew the magic words for accepting the facts of your life (feel free to start singing the theme song if you are a child of the eighties). All I know to do is ask God to help me, over and over again, to accept my reality and to find my way back to faith, hope, and love.

Once again the Examen is generous in what it offers. Gratitude assists us in acceptance. Look to the gifts of your day to lessen the blow of what is difficult to accept. Humans are such all or nothing creatures. We struggle with the in between. When you are aware of the good, it's easier to take the bad. If you can avoid thinking your life is all good or all bad, acceptance comes more naturally.

---

61   D. Linn, S. Linn, M. Linn, *Sleeping with Bread: Holding What Gives You Life*, 1.

ALL THE MORE

- Use the above questions during the "Review Your Day" portion of the Examen. Ask for light to see where you are as you reflect on the moments of your day.
- James Baldwin said, "Not everything that is faced can be changed. But nothing can be changed until it is faced." Pray for the courage to face your reality head on.
- Ask God to remind you often where you are headed—toward faith, hope, and love—and to reveal to you the path to get there today.

day 23: character

"Character—the willingness to accept responsibility for one's own
life—is the source from which self-respect springs."
— JOAN DIDION

In her 2009 novel, *Home Safe*, Elizabeth Berg tells the story of a fiftyish, recently widowed author named Helen Ames. Toward the end of the novel, after much upheaval and change, Helen is given the opportunity to write a review for the work of a fellow author, Margot, a woman who has disparaged Helen's work in the past. Helen vacillates between bitterness over Margot's (unfair) criticism and admiration of Margot's manuscript. After a sleepless night, she comes to this conclusion:

She will craft the best blurb she can for Margot's book. She will try to help an author who detests her, *because of the home she wants to build inside herself,* because of how she wants to live. In the end, to forgive, to tell the truth, to honor what is worthy of admiration, hurts less than the alternative. And there it is: if she offers words of praise to Margot, it will free her from the stinging criticism Margot offered her. Odd to think it works that way, but for Helen, it does.[62]

The *home she wants to build inside herself* is one of character. The *Collins Dictionary* defines character this way: "If you say that someone has character, you mean that they have the ability to deal effectively with difficult, unpleasant, or dangerous situations."[63] And for Helen, wrapped up in effectively dealing with the unpleasant situation with Margot is being able to live with herself. Helen makes the decision that allows her to sleep at night. She settles on who she knows herself to be—even when the situation itself provides an easy out. In her choice to write a positive book review for an enemy, Helen chooses who she wants to be—how she wants to live.

You make a life with every decision you make. You choose who you want to be with each step you take. Walking with such intention and purpose requires constant vigilance and attention. It is the opposite of floating on a lazy river or being carried by the tides. Daily events and moments can act like a river or tide for our souls. I know I get caught up in the happenings of my day and forget which way I'm going. I am no more aware of my nearness to God than I am to my feelings about a particular situation when I'm being pulled in multiple directions.

> I choose today the home I want to build inside myself.

Do you remember when you learned in grade school that an object in motion stays in motion unless acted upon by an out-

---

62 Elizabeth Berg, *Home Safe*: A Novel (New York: Ballantine Books, 2009), 242.

63 "Character Definition and Meaning," *Collins English Dictionary* (HarperCollins Publishers Ltd), https://www.collinsdictionary.com/us/dictionary/english/character.

side force? I (when I'm going with the flow of what happens on a Tuesday) am like the object in motion. Worry has an energy. Gossip, negativity, hurry, fear—all have a propulsive force that keeps me moving away from God (the awareness of God—God never moves). I am subject to the natural laws of inertia unless I am "acted upon by an outside force." The outside force that most often disrupts my current state is the Presence I receive from being still as I practice the Examen.

My only hope when I'm caught in the tides of unexpected news or overwhelming emotion is to carefully examine my responses to these circumstances. The Examen invites me to consider if what is moving me is what brings me life—or death.

I know what it feels like to be Helen, who rode the wave of several negative encounters with Margot and felt pulled to the obvious next move—to return hate for hate. It is the way of things. Only silence and reflection pull me out of the flow and remind me who I want to be and what brings me closer to God. When I connect to God's presence and love for me in the Examen, I find what I need to make the choices that lead to the life I want to build for myself and those around me.

How I wish that you and I could develop character without suffering and setbacks. It just isn't my experience—or that of anyone I know well. I was twenty-six years old when my first child was born. Apart from normal ups and downs, I had yet to endure the kind of suffering that produces endurance; endurance, character; and character, hope that Paul wrote about in Romans. And I wanted to. I wanted to be ONE with Jesus in suffering.

I decided that I would have a natural childbirth in order to experience pain. (I'm rolling my own eyes.) I made a mix CD (yes, I did) of all the songs that sang mournfully about the suffering and death of Jesus to play during the birth. Mind you, I got pregnant easily and enjoyed a normal and healthy pregnancy (I bypassed an enormous amount of suffering with those two realities). I was all set to meet Jesus in suffering. Spoiler alert: My nine-hour uncomplicated labor did not create endurance and character—even with my mix CD playing in the background.

You know what did? Parenting that child over the next nineteen years. Noticing when he was two, five, eight, twelve, and fifteen years old that he wasn't like the other kids. Hearing hard news about what might complicate his life. Having a friend tell you that she wouldn't let her son play with mine anymore because she didn't want my son's anger rubbing off on her son. Pulling him out of a school I'd spent years praying he would attend because being there was breaking his spirit. Watching kids make fun of him. Worrying and wondering about his future. Choosing every day to love that kid with everything I had—even when I was embarrassed or scared or worried beyond belief.

As a kid, I came home every day from school and watched *The Oprah Winfrey Show* at 4 p.m. Say what you want about Oprah, but she introduced me to people and stories I would have never encountered in my small town in Pennsylvania. I remember being thirteen or fourteen years old the first time I heard her quote Maya Angelou, "People may not remember what you did or what you said, but they always remember how you made them feel."

When both Oprah and Maya encouraged us viewers to smile at children when they walked into the room—to let them feel our love for them—I imagined my own unborn children. I never forgot their wisdom. God showed me the way, all those years ago, to walk with my son—with love and delight. God reminded me daily in the Examen how love and delight led to life for both of us. "You may encounter many defeats, but you must not be defeated. In fact, it may be necessary to encounter the defeats, so *you can know who you are, what you can rise from,* how you can still come out of it," says Maya Angelou (again, and always—never too much Maya).

There are things I know about myself that I wouldn't know if I didn't have that particular son. Things I only saw because God showed me day after day the path forward—one that led me closer to God. So many times, I thought for sure we would all be washed out to sea by the struggles and challenges we faced with him. But the still, quiet voice of God—revealed in the love of friends, family, and teachers and in the delight of rivers, trees, and birds—gently and lovingly moved us closer and closer to life. Today, that young man rises. He stands tall and proud. I'm next to him—hopeful and grateful.

ALL THE MORE

- People often say, "Dig down deep" when you are in a tough spot. What do you find when you go deep inside yourself? Give thanks for the gifts that help you endure. What do you long to see more of? Ask God to grow that in you.

- Rumi said, "The wound is the place where the Light enters you." Have you experienced light in your own wounds—your own suffering? What did God use to remind you of Presence and Love?

- Is there something you are avoiding because it's hard or uncomfortable? Ask God to help you be who you want to be in that situation.

- Draw or write down characteristics of the home you want to build inside yourself. What does it look like? What elements does it possess?

day 24: serve

"So whatever you wish that others would do to you,
do also to them, for this is the Law and the Prophets."
— MATTHEW 7:12 (ESV)

As a freshman in college, I read the book *Savage Inequalities: Children in America's Schools* by Jonathan Kozol. The book, written in 1991, discusses the disparities in education between schools of different classes and races. It is based on Kozol's observations of various classrooms in the public school systems of East St. Louis, Chicago, New York City, Camden, Cincinnati, and Washington, DC. I read the book in the context of a freshman seminar called "Just Desserts." We discussed what people deserve or have a right to in American society. Most of the topics we covered I had never even considered.

We had one junior high and one high school for the entire county I grew up in. I remember one private Catholic school that went through sixth grade and one private Christian high school. Very few people I knew went to either. It never occurred to me that things could be different for other kids my age. I took for granted that if you wanted a good education, you got it, and if you wanted to go to college, you figured out a way to pay for it. The fact that some kids received less of an education or less education because of their class or race was mind-blowing to me.

I believed the author's premise that racism existed in America, but I did not think it could infect the church. I am one of those Christians who had a definitive before and after conversion experience and, in my way of thinking then, the "after" contained none of the bad of the before. (Bless my idealistic and naive heart, right? It was such a far fall back down.)

I just assumed that Christians were different, a.k.a. not racist or classist, and that people who loved God loved everyone equally without prejudice. Somehow, I missed that the only Christians are actual humans who are both good and bad AND that the church is made of those same complicated people. (I figured it out soon enough.) Books like *Divided by Faith* by Michael O. Emerson and Christian Smith quickly disabused me of my privileged Pollyanna notions. *The Color of Compromise* by Jemar Tisby, a more recent addition to the study of the church and racism, continues to expose the ugly truth.

When I think back to those days when I didn't know that lovers of God could be haters of the people God made, I feel amazement and grief. I wish I didn't know now what I didn't know then. AND I'm grateful to be wide awake to the realities that so many of my brothers and sisters in the faith experience as people of color. Now that I've seen the wounds caused by racism, I can't look away. I'm compelled to act—for justice and for greater faith, hope, and love among people who oppress and those who are oppressed.

One of the values of the Jesuits is "becoming a person for others." To be a person for others means responding to pain, tragedy, and suffering in the capacity of a servant in order to meet another's needs.

Knowing and sensing God's love is only the beginning of the spiritual journey. Spreading the love, healing, and hope you've found in Jesus "to the ends of the earth" is the daily walk of faith for the lover of God.

Author and theologian Frederick Buechner wrote, "The place God calls you to is the place where your deep gladness and the world's deep hunger meet." Deep gladness to me is that soul knowing that I'm loved and cared for by God. When that bumps up against what is wrong in the world, I know I have something to give.

Over the years, my commitment to pursue racial justice and equity is confirmed repeatedly in the Examen. I've noticed that these are the stories that catch my attention, that bring tears to my eyes, that cause the anger to rise within me—over and over again. What is it that captures you? Where do you feel called to serve others? Begin to pay attention in the Examen to what causes you to feel anger, fear, or shame.

Perhaps there is fortitude you can bring to the fight for justice, companionship you can offer to those doing hard things, or welcome you can extend to those who have lost their way. Offer your tears, your emotions, and your deep gladness to God. You will be shown who needs it.

Let the Examen guide you to the fulfillment of Micah 6:8 in your own life. "But he's already made it plain how to live, what to do, what God is looking for in men and women. It's quite simple: Do what is fair and just to your neighbor, be compassionate and loyal in your love, and don't take yourself too seriously—take God seriously."

ALL THE MORE

An Examen for These Days

Thank you.

Thank you that you are near to all you have made. All are made in Your image in love, with love, and because of love. Thank you that You are close to me and You love me.

Show me.

Show me every place You are present and active on this earth that is groaning to be remade. Show me in everyone Your commitment to make all things new. Shine the light of truth into the darkest of places and expose every lie that holds me, your people, and your creation captive.

Let me see.

Let me see what has yet to be renewed in faith, love, and hope in every system, structure, institution, and group. Open my eyes to the ones you love who suffer injustice, oppression, and hate. Where have I ignored Your call to act on behalf of others? Where has my own comfort or privilege blinded me to the needs of and unfair practices against others?

Let me see Your heart for the victims of oppression and for those who oppress. Open my eyes to my own soul. How am I really doing? Help me talk to you, God, about the anger, sadness, fear, and hurt that lives in me as a result of the racism, division, ignorance, and apathy I witness. Let me see that You are with me in it.

Forgive me.

Forgive me for where I have given darkness free reign—through my actions or my silence. Forgive me for my chosen ignorance and weary resignation. Forgive me for thinking that You've left it this way on purpose, that You're not able or willing to help, and that You'll never intervene. I am worn out and tired. Forgive me for forgetting that it was never my battle alone to fight—that it was never my name at stake, but Yours.

Lead me.

Lead me down every road that ends in peace. Lead me into faith, hope, and love. Lead me to pursue justice and equity for all You have made—and give me the strength, stamina, and vision to do so. Let me follow the lead of Jesus who chose humility and solidarity with the weak. Most of all, lead me today into Your presence to receive the faith, hope, and love I need to keep on going.

day 25: now

"Give your entire attention to what God is doing right now, and
don't get worked up about what may or may not happen tomorrow."
— Matthew 6:34

When my kids were small, well-meaning moms of older kids said to me, "Enjoy this! The days may be long, but the years are short." I would offer a tight smile and promise to squeeze the life out of them—I mean the moment—while I had the chance. I know what they were trying to say, and they were right. I miss the chubby hand resting on my forearm. I miss the snuggly boy who just woke up from the nap. I miss always knowing where they are and what they are doing at all times.

When I was a kid, I couldn't wait to go back to school. Once I had my first day of school outfit and school supplies ready to go, the days couldn't pass quickly enough. Within a couple of months, I was pining for the first day of summer—for warm weather and pool days. I spent grade school wishing I was in high school and in high school wishing I was in college. I spent college wondering if I would get married and once married, wondering if I would have children. When I had children, I wondered what they—and I—would be when we all grew up.

I think I was in my thirties before I had any real sense of what Emily Dickinson meant when she wrote, "Forever is composed of nows." I missed so many nows waiting for my forever when my responses to my nows were actually defining who I would be and what my life would become. So, I try. I try to live in the moment. To be present. To live the day that's in front of me.

It sounds like bumper sticker theology, but Jesus had a lot to say about keeping our hearts in the now. He said don't worry about tomorrow. He taught us to pray for daily bread. When Mary anointed his feet with expensive oil, he said she's doing it because I am with you now—and won't be *like this* forever. Jesus said in so many words, "Be with me now."

The Examen insists that you focus on the present because you bring *what is happening now* to God. There is a time to go back and consider your past. There is a time to think ahead and pray toward the future. But your forever is made with each and every moment of your today. As Henry David Thoreau said, "You must live in the present, launch yourself on every wave, find your eternity in each moment. Fools stand on their island of opportunities and look toward another land. There is no other land; there is no other life but this, or the like of this."

What does God want to say right now about your life? What gifts does God want to give? The First Principle and Foundation includes this sentence, "All the things in this world are gifts of God, presented to us so that we can know God more easily and make a return of love more readily." Something or someone today is there to show you the goodness and mercy of God and to help you love God more easily. Don't miss it!

"Be present in all things and thankful for all things," said Maya Angelou. To be present IS to be thankful. The God who wants to know you and wants you to know Him is showing you today where He is in your world. My friend and fellow Enneagram coach, Vanessa Sadler, shared her experience of praying the Examen with me. I'm quoting her email, in its entirety, because it's such a beautiful example of being with God in her present moments.

I sit in a comfortable chair and take several deep breaths, opening myself to what God envisions for this time. I close my eyes and start at the beginning of my day, allowing brief scenes and snapshots to roll through my mind like an old movie reel. As each image rolls, I pray an honest prayer. One sentence. No more, no less.

When I first woke to my son at my bedside... God, I'd like more rest.

I didn't want to get out of bed just yet... God, I feel so lazy.

I was upset about something... God, I feel so powerless.

As I become aware of my own self-talk and judgment, I stop the movie. My inclination is to critique my own process of the exercise. Rather than abandon my time, I choose to lean in and remain open to anything God might have to show me. Closing my eyes again, I breathe and allow the images to continue.

I played a game with two of my children and grinned at their giggles... Is this how you delight in me, God?

My daughter shows me her artwork... God, her eyes are so kind, her touch so sweet.

My son tells me a story... He has Your passion, God.

The clouds as I drive on the highway... God, you are a true Artist.

A phone call with a friend... God, thank you that I am seen.

The briefest of moments to myself... I notice myself breathe deep and release... You orchestrated that moment, God. Thank you.

A good meal... God, you provide.

I notice a patch of dead grass in the yard. My husband says, "It'll live again"... Death to life. Over and over. God, you are here.

I wish I could say that I responded just like this as each of these moments happened in real time. I didn't. Sure, there were times when I relished my child's eyes or paused just long enough to look at the clouds, but I didn't have the ongoing awareness of God in my experience, communing with me. Only as I experienced in the Examen and re-flected in "reel" time did I have the presence of mind to invite God into the scene. I was warmed by the exercise and came away much more attentive to the fact that the nearness of God is palpable and available for me always. I end my time in gratitude for a God who exists outside of time, and that I am permitted and invited to grow my sensitivity both retroactively and futuristically. Grateful that this invitation is actually an invitation to be more present in each moment.

ALL THE MORE

- Where do you tend to get stuck? Obsessing over your past or worrying about your future? When you catch yourself doing what you do, gently bring your thoughts back to this moment. Remind yourself that God meant for it to be easy—knowing and loving God. Ask to see, know, and believe this to be true.
- "What day is it?" asked Pooh. "It's today," squeaked Piglet. "My favorite day," said Pooh." (A.A. Milne) What can you give thanks for today? To be present IS to be thankful.
- What did "daily bread" look like for you today? Ask God to fill and calm your soul with today's provision.

day 26: together

"We're all just walking each other home."
— RAM DASS

We are relational beings. We are made that way—by a relational God. We know this because, for whatever reason, God did not choose to identify as a singular being. God chose to reveal himself as Trinitarian—which means made up of three persons—the Father, the Son, and the Spirit.

God is not lonely and not dependent on you for company. You weren't created to fill a need. You were created for relationships—with other humans and with God the Three in One. In the beginning, Genesis 1:26 (NIV) recounts how God said, "Let us make human beings in our own image, in our likeness..." God is already in a relationship within God's own being. You are created for connection and response to the invitation to be in a relationship with God. And everything God made is meant to help you respond with love to God's invitation.

All of your relationships on earth—with yourself, with others, with God—are life's most important teachers. Given to you to prepare you for an eternity in connection with everything and everyone God made. You learn by making friends, going to work, getting married, having kids, tending a garden, and walking a dog. Your purpose isn't to exist by yourself in perfection. Your good purpose is to take your God-given place as part of the whole thing. When God saw *everything* He made, indeed, it was very good.

> *Tov* is the Hebrew word for "good," but the word does not refer only to the goodness of the object itself; it also refers to the ties between things. In the Hebrew conception of the world, all of creation is connected. The well-being of the whole depends on the well-being of each individual part. The Hebrews conception of goodness was different than the Greeks. The Greeks located perfection within the object itself. A thing or person strove toward perfection. The Hebrew's understood goodness to be located *between* things. As a result, the original hearers would have understood *tov* to refer to the goodness of the ties and relationships between things in creation.[64]

So, if goodness is found between things, then good work in the world involves cultivating good relationships with others. Easier said than done—especially in our particular cultural climate. But it is your birthright and your calling to develop connections with all God has made. And as the First Principle and Foundation reminds us, "All the things in this world are also created because of God's love and they become a context of gifts, presented to us so that we can know God more easily and make a return of love more readily."

---

64 Harper, 30–31.

I don't know about you, but I'm not great at seeing myself clearly. I'm not talking about what I see in the mirror. I do, in fact, see that my eyeliner is smudged or my hair is frizzy. What I struggle to see is my goodness. Not the deeds I do or things I accomplish but the image of God in me. I can easily miss the buds of goodness sprouting up in my work or the flower that bloomed right there in that desert of a situation.

That's why I have friends. Dinah Maria Mulock Craik said, "A friend is one to whom one may pour out the contents of one's heart, chaff and grain together, knowing that gentle hands will take and sift it, keep what is worth keeping, and with a breath of kindness, blow the rest away." I need my friends to spot the goodness, hold onto it with me, and help me let go of the things that lead me away from God.

I have a friend I talk to most days. I've known her since I was twenty-three. There isn't anything she doesn't know—good and bad—about me. Sometimes I don't know what I think or feel about something until I've said it out loud to her. And sometimes, I don't notice what God is doing in my life until she points it out. As we've matured in our relationship with each other and in our own with God, our daily talks feel almost like praying the Examen to me. I tell her what I'm thankful for, I ask for direction, I reflect on my day, I confess when I was an idiot, and I look ahead to tomorrow.

When I consider why our daily talks mean so much to me, I'm reminded of a line from the 2004 movie *Shall We Dance?* starring Richard Gere and Susan Sarandon. When asked why she wants to be married, Sarandon's character replies:

We need a witness to our lives. There's a billion people on the planet... I mean what does any one life really mean?

But in a marriage, you're promising to care about everything. The good things, the bad things, the terrible things, the mundane things... all of it, all of the time, every day. You're saying "Your life will not go unnoticed because I will notice it. Your life will not go un-witnessed because I will be your witness."

She is talking about a marriage relationship, but I believe it applies to any relationship that helps us see and be seen—a partner, a friend, a parent, a sibling. We all need someone to witness our lives. To care about the minute details and sort them with us. The goodness is between things and between people who have agreed to witness one another's life.

I offer the Examen as a prayer practice to almost all who come to me for spiritual direction (if I didn't, I'm so sorry—I'm writing this book for you!). Last year, I decided to offer a spiritual direction group that focused on praying the Examen. Each member committed to praying on their own and meeting monthly to share their insights and experiences.

Something magical happened between those of us in the group. We witnessed growth, hope ebbing and flowing, and the movements of a person's soul over time. We were given God's eyes—for those precious hours—to see that person's heart as God does. We reflected back to each other what we heard and shared images or words of encouragement that came to mind as each person spoke. It felt easy to know and love God (and each other!) in the context of witnessing each other's lives.

There are passages that the soul can only take alone. And journeys that you won't survive if you try to go it alone. Find someone to share the interior of your being with. Watch what happens when you put it all on the table in front of someone else. I bet you'll be surprised by what they notice in the dump of your day. You'll know you've found a soul friend when you leave your time with them feeling closer to God, closer to yourself, and closer to fine (I couldn't help myself—the Indigo Girls were everything in college).

ALL THE MORE

- I think David Whyte knows something about having a soul friend, "But no matter the medicinal virtues of being a true friend or sustaining a long close relationship with another, the ultimate touchstone of friendship is not improvement, neither of the other nor of the self, the ultimate touchstone is witness, the privilege of having been seen by someone and the equal privilege of being granted the sight of the essence of another, to have walked with them and to have believed in them, and sometimes just to have accompanied them for however brief a span, on a journey impossible to accomplish alone."[65] Think about your relationships. In which have you felt the pressure to change the other or change for the other person? What would it look like to shift the focus to being a witness? To asking for a witness?
- What do you need help seeing in your life today? Ask God to open your eyes—and to provide another pair of eyes to see with you.

---

65 David Whyte, *Consolations: The Solace, Nourishment and Underlying Meaning of Everyday Words* (Edinburgh: Canongate Books Ltd., 2019).

day 27: inner freedom

"To keep our faces toward change and behave like free spirits in the presence of fate, is strength undefeatable."
— HELEN KELLER

In *The Spiritual Exercises*, Ignatius wrote extensively about the decision-making process. Many of his ideas you still use today. While many attribute the invention of the pro/con list to Benjamin Franklin, Ignatius taught the practice 200 years before Franklin ever wrote about it.

What is unique about Ignatius's approach to making a list of the positive and negative aspects of a decision is the idea of inner freedom. Inner freedom is simply the freedom to choose the way of God. Oftentimes we come to decisions with our minds already made up or with the expectations of others central to our focus.

Freedom, as Ignatius thought about it, had less to do with being freed from something (although surely we all need to let go of what keeps us from love) and more to do with being freed FOR something—free to love and serve God and others.

One of the words Ignatius used often to indicate freedom is "indifference." In this case, being indifferent doesn't mean apathy or unconcerned but open or open-minded. George E. Ganss, SJ, defines indifference this way, "Undetermined to one thing or option rather than another; impartial; unbiased; with decision suspended until the reasons for a wise choice are learned; still undecided."

Think of the story of the rich young man in Matthew 19. He comes to Jesus and asks what he needs to do to get eternal life. Jesus tells him to follow the commandments. The man basically says, "Been there, done that—what's next?" I like the Message translation for the next part, "If you want to give it all you've got," Jesus replied, "go sell your possessions; give everything to the poor. All your wealth will then be in heaven. Then come follow me." That was the last thing the young man expected to hear. And so, crestfallen, he walked away. He was holding on tight to a lot of things, and he couldn't bear to let go.

The young man did not possess indifference. He came to Jesus with an expectation of what he thought Jesus would say. And when Jesus told him what was needed, he wasn't open to it because he didn't expect it.

How many times have you come to Jesus like the rich young ruler? You want to give—unless it's giving that. You want to serve—unless it's serving there. You want to love—unless it's loving them.

This brings us to another word that sheds light on the presence or absence of inner freedom: attachments. Margaret Silf identifies both positive attachments and negative attachments—"things I excessively [desire] to have or to be, and things I excessively [desire] to avoid."[66] (If you're thinking this sounds a lot like the Core

---

66   Silf, 142.

Desire and Core Fear of your Enneagram type, then you're on the right track.)[67]

The young man not only had expectations of what he imagined Jesus would tell him to do but also a positive attachment to his wealth and a negative attachment to poverty. As an Enneagram One, I have a positive attachment to being right and a negative attachment to being wrong. When I come to a decision, these attachments affect my ability to hear from God because I've already decided one outcome is more right or wrong than another. I'm not actually open to what God might say because my attachments prevent me from being indifferent. I lack the inner freedom to choose the option God lays before me.

And my version of right and wrong is not necessarily the same as God's. If I have a positive attachment to appearing non-materialistic, then I might think living in the "fancy" area of town is wrong. My opinion is subjective but may prevent me from moving where God wants me to live.

When you bring your awareness of these concepts to the Examen, you open the door to better decision-making and lasting transformation. I know you've had something you've held out to God and begged, "Please show me what to do here." If you're like me, you've asked in tears, on repeat. And when days turn to weeks turn to months, you start to wonder if God listens or cares. I say this with all the gentleness of a butterfly kiss—you might not be able to see what God is doing because you have a shortage of inner freedom. Your attachments may be obscuring your view and blocking your indifference.

Two fruitful questions I ask in the Examen are: What today has been life-giving to me? What today has been life-draining? My

---

67   For a list of Enneagram Core Desires and Fears, see the chart in the Appendix.

spiritual director used to remind me, "Follow the life" or "Follow the light." She meant that if I followed the crumbs of what gave me life, I would find the gifts God was giving and the purposes for which I was made. Always walk toward whatever brings you life and light—a desire for God and an increase in faith, hope, and love.

On the other hand, you can follow the trail right over a cliff when you focus on what drains your life. If you attend to the people, events, circumstances, or ambitions that drain the life from your soul, you might find yourself eye to eye with one of your positive or negative attachments. And you just might find the blinders that keep you from noticing the faith, hope, and love God is offering to you.

I've been a spiritual director for many years now. The work of listening with another soul for their own heart and God's voice is one of the most life-giving practices I engage in on any given day. It does not, however, pay a lot of bills. Sometime last winter, I noticed that our fluctuating finances—and my insistence on ignoring them—caused a significant energy drain on my soul. I had half-heartedly pursued full-time work in the past and even got close to accepting a position the year before.

I prayed for guidance and believed myself to be faithfully seeking it from God. My pursuit of full-time work continued to surface in the practice of the Examen, and I needed to get to the bottom of my reluctance. I asked God to show me why I was avoiding full-time work outside the home. Apart from loving spiritual direction (which I will do in some fashion as long as God gives me breath), I discovered that one of my motivations was an unhealthy attachment to other people's expectations.

Early on in my faith journey, I received the spoken and unspoken message that the best and highest good for a woman was to marry and have children. A woman's calling, schedule, and dreams come second to those of her family's. "Available" and "present" grew over the years into positive attachments—I am only a good wife and mother if I am available and present at all times. (It certainly didn't help that I had a husband who traveled extensively for work. Isn't that usually the case? Our personalities + half-truths + circumstances create a dangerous cocktail.) The negative attachment was to being away from the home and inflexible—and being seen as a bad mother. God and I spent some time healing the wounds caused from those ideas.

When I approached the question of full-time work again, I was as close to inner freedom as I ever had been. At just the right time, I mentioned my search to a friend and she passed along an opportunity. I applied, interviewed and accepted the job within two weeks. The doors were flying open and I had peace (consolation) that God was moving me into this new role. I started my job on March 16, 2020. Guess how many days I worked? Three. They let me go on March 18 due to office closures and Coronavirus.

Two months later, I got the idea for this book and chose not to go back to that job when they reopened the office later that summer. I have no idea why it all worked out the way it did—why I had to go through that whole process of getting and losing the job. But I do know I have more freedom now than I did then. And I'm being transformed FOR something—for greater faith, hope, and love—if only I will see.

ALL THE MORE

- Go back to the story of the rich young man. What expectations do you bring to your requests of God? What attachments—positive or negative—block your ability to be indifferent?

- Ask God to remind you of a time when you made a decision based on inner freedom. What did it feel like? What was the fruit of the decision? Now ask to be shown a time when you made a decision based on a preconceived idea—something you had to have or something you had to avoid. What was the fruit of the decision?

- Ignatius used the image of a "pointer of a balance" to symbolize indifference. Picture a metal scale in the grocery store that weighs vegetables, cheese, or meat. When nothing is on the scale, the arrow points straight up to zero. Imagine yourself as the arrow pointing straight up—not leaning to one side or the other. Ask for the grace to come to God with indifference when you face a decision. Feel the weightlessness, the freedom of an empty scale. Experience the openness, the possibility of what God wants to do next in your life. God is transforming you FOR something. Ask to know what it is.

- If you know your Enneagram type, spend some time contemplating how your core desire and core fear interfere with your ability to receive what God might be offering. How do they sway you toward or away from God? For a list of desires and fears, see the chart in the Appendix of the book.

day 28: practice

"For the things we have to learn before we can do them,
we learn by doing them."

— ARISTOTLE

I tried yoga for the first time over ten years ago. I found Down-ward-Facing Dog nearly impossible to hold and Dolphin a complete nightmare (I'm still terrible at it). I toppled to one side each time I got into Tree pose and failed to reach my fingers to my toes. The instructor referred to my awkward movements as "your yoga practice" though, and something about that allowed me to keep trying. I've been practicing yoga a long time now, and my yoga practice is indeed my own.

I have more balance and flexibility than I did in the beginning, but my tight shoulders still make certain poses difficult. I don't do headstands (thank you, car wreck of 1999) or have straight legs in Boat pose (bless you, tight hamstrings). But I've learned to show up and take from my yoga practice exactly what I need.

I imagine you are comfortable thinking about practice in the context of your body. Anything not a game or match in sports is considered practice. It's understood that the point of practice is to improve, to work toward something better.

I bet you're also okay with the application of practice to your mind. Schools offer practice ACTS and SATS, practice math problems, and Sudoku. If you continue to use a part of your mind for the same skill, you train your minds to get better at it or retain its function.

Do you know what might make you squirm a little? The thought that your soul needs practice. That your relationship with God needs practice. That prayer requires practice.

I thought I should just know things about God, the Bible, and prayer right out of the gate. And not growing up as a Christian, I was always behind the eight-ball. It was made very clear to me that I needed to have a quiet time that included prayer and Bible study, but I don't know that I picked up the specifics on how to do it. So, I figured it out for myself. And I don't remember anyone telling me it might take time or practice to feel more natural.

I think that's another reason I like being a spiritual director so much. In spiritual direction training, everything is referred to as a spiritual practice. I may have been introduced to this phrase before my training but I didn't latch onto it until then. I read whole books about contemplative prayer, and the assumption is that it takes years to pray it well.

I was given this quote by Francis de Sales years ago and it is balm to my soul each time I read it: "If the heart wanders or is distracted, bring it back to the point quite gently and replace it tenderly in its Master's presence. And even if you did nothing during the whole of your hour but bring your heart back and place it again in Our Lord's presence, though it went away every time you brought it back, your hour would be very well employed."

What do you tell your heart when it wanders during prayer? How do you speak to it? If you're like me, I imagine you get a bit frustrated and say, "Pull yourself together, heart!" You would not be alone. I gave the Examen to a new directee and the following month she said in exasperation, "I prayed it a whole week and nothing happened!" She was so genuinely disturbed that she didn't master a brand-new prayer practice in one week. I wonder if she would have felt that way about trying a new sport or learning a new subject.

Julia—a friend, a contemplative, a counselor, and a spiritual director—describes her own journey in praying the Examen. She writes:

> All those years of wanting so desperately for the Examen to be THAT prayer that everyone said it was—the key that would unlock God's presence in my life. Every book I read, every story I heard of someone else's transformation by the practice would strengthen my inner narrative that there must be something wrong with me that I wasn't experiencing what others described.
>
> Recently, I received an email offering a group experience with the Examen I felt a stirring in my heart to join. It was that invitational energy, not the grit and determination I usually brought to the practice. The first night as we introduced ourselves and shared why we were there, I responded that my intention was to finally wrestle the Examen to the ground. I was then invited into silence. And as clear as day, I heard God singing to me the words of a song by Lonestar—the gist of which is I'm already here in everything around you. There was nothing I had to do to commune with God—no vigilant examination of

my heart, no penance, no wrestling match. He's already there—always has been, always will be.

Julia's words highlight so well how "soul practice" differs from other kinds of practice. In every other form of training you are attempting to improve, to know more, to be better. With the soul, the goal is to grow more comfortable, feel more natural, and experience "home" in our relationship with God. And some of that is work you can't do, only God can. It is a gift to feel the presence of God in prayer. It is a grace to hear God's voice. The practice for you is to keep showing up, to keep gently bringing your heart before God's.

I like to read about the brain. I think some of what scientists are learning about how it works is helpful. "The old adage we usually hear is that 'practice makes perfect.' Based on what we know about neuroplasticity and deliberate practice, we should rephrase that to read, 'practice makes permanent.' Remember that it is not about being perfect, but about creating new neural pathways that shift your default... programming as you grow in awareness and skill."[68]

Isn't that amazing? Your brain can build new roads on which new information can permanently travel. What if you chose to practice the presence of God in the Examen? Your brain could actually rewire itself to think about where God is in your days. You could permanently change your awareness to seek God's voice.

It's possible. Practice *makes* it possible. Possibility brings you to the inner freedom of being able to say yes to the good movement toward faith, hope, and love. I may not be a brain expert,

---

68 Zaretta Hammond, *Culturally Responsive Teaching and the Brain* (Thousand Oaks, CA: Corwin, 2015).

but I do feel encouraged to keep showing up to God in the Examen with this kind of hope on the horizon.

ALL THE MORE

- Notice your responses to yourself when your heart wanders in prayer—or you fall asleep! Choose to return to God's presence without judgment. Let it be enough today that you returned.

- Can you relate to Julia's attempt to "wrestle the Examen to the ground" when it comes to spiritual practice? Instead of winning or improving, think about building a home. And even if you never finish the whole house, you get to spend part of every day doing good work building it.

- Ask for what you need from God to trust the slow work of learning to pray.

day 29: desires

"It would seem that Our Lord finds our desires not too strong, but too weak. We are half-hearted creatures, fooling about with drink, sex, and ambition when infinite joy is offered us, like an ignorant child who wants to go on making mud pies in a slum because he cannot imagine what is meant by the offer of a holiday at the sea. We are far too easily pleased."

— C.S. LEWIS, *THE WEIGHT OF GLORY*

A leper tells Jesus, "If you want to, you can cleanse me." Jesus responds, "I want to. Be clean." (Mark 1:40–41) Later, Jesus asks a blind beggar, "What can I do for you?" (Mark 10:51) You are a creature who wants. There is no getting around it. You may want chocolate, time with a friend, financial stability, health, intimate love, and purpose. You also may want domination, revenge, and destruction. Christians have a complicated relationship with their wants, or desires as the Scriptures often refer to them. If you want too much, desire can be dangerous. If you want too little, desire can be squashed and flattened.

In her book *Inner Compass*, Margaret Silf writes about desires as having directional energy. They move us. She identifies two directions of movement: down and deep and up and out. Silf labels the desires that move down and deep root desires. She further explains that root desires are "desires that delve down deep, seeking hold and nourishment and security." Examples of root desires include a desire for a safe home, a peaceful world, people who care for you, and health—physical, mental, and spiritual.

Silf calls desires that move up and out branch desires. They are "desires that urge me to express myself, to spread out my arms and my heart to the world around me and to my friends and loved ones; to reach out to those things that embody light and warmth for me—those things that delight and warm my heart." Branch desires might look like a desire for meaningful work, a desire to "mourn with those who mourn," or a desire to be moved by art or music. Root desires move us deeper into our basic needs and branch desires move us up and out of ourselves—toward others and God.[69]

Root or branch desires are neither good nor bad. Ignatius does, however, distinguish between desires that give and desires that take. He calls giving desires "ordered" and taking desires "disordered."

- Ordered desires "expand us without diminishing the other. They draw us into a creative relationship with what lies beyond ourselves without tempting us to try to possess it." Ordered implies that things are as they should be—the object of desire remains unspoiled (love, hope, joy) and you grow in faith, hope, and love by being drawn into its orbit.
- Disordered desires "tempt us to suck things into ourselves and result in the diminishment of the desired object." Dis-

---

69 Silf, 110.

ordered implies things are not as they should be—you get bloated and the object of your desire shrinks or disappears.[70]

Silf uses the imagery of a bee and a spider to further explain the difference between ordered and disordered desires. Spiders show us what disordered desires look like in that they take in everything that comes into the spider's web. The spider grows but destroys what it consumes. The spider takes or possesses its desire.

A disordered desire might be one in which you desire to live out your dreams through your children. The children are consumed in your dreams for them—you get fatter on their awards and successes—but they shrink as individual selves.

The bee on the other hand is drawn to the nectar of the flower. The bee gives to its desire (pollination) even as it receives pollen from the flower. Both the bee and the flower benefit from the relationship.

An ordered desire might be a desire for good work in the world. As a nurse, you give care and help to your patients and you receive back satisfaction and purpose.

Desires require time and effort to sort out. The Examen can help you put your finger on what it is you want and the methods you are using to get it. By reviewing your day in the Spirit's gaze, you begin to see your movement toward what you desire.

You can notice if you are approaching situations as a bee or a spider. You can pay attention to how you give and take. Above all, you can let God draw you toward your deepest desires as you identify the ones that occupy your time and energy.

---

70 Silf, 128–129.

In Ignatian spirituality, the deepest desire is the one we have for God—to know and be known. All other desires point to this one. William Barry says:

> Prayer is a conscious relationship with God. Just as we spend time with friends because we love them and care for them, we spend time in prayer because we love God and want to be with God. Created out of love, we are drawn by the desire for "we know not what," for union with the ultimate Mystery, who alone will satisfy our deepest longing. That desire, we can say, is the Holy Spirit of God dwelling in our hearts, drawing us to the perfect fulfillment for which we were created— namely, community with the Trinity. That desire draws us toward a more and more intimate union with God.[71]

Everything you want or long for signals your soul's deepest ache for intimacy with your Creator. Whatever rings all the bells inside of you is your connection to your hearts deepest desire. The Examen helps you remember that all desire is desire for God by placing all the feelings, energies, events, and circumstances of the day in God's hands. All is done before God and because of God. And what you *really* want is to know and be known by that God.

---

71   William A. Barry, *God's Passionate Desire* (Chicago: Loyola Press, 2008).

ALL THE MORE

- Make a list of your root and branch desires. Notice what desires go deep and nourish you and which lift you up and out into the world God made.
- Use the imagery of a spider and bee to identify a disordered and ordered desire in your life.
- In Elizabeth J. Canham's *Heart Whispers*, she explores obedience as waiting:[72] "What kind of life does my heart want? I find no easy answers to that question, but I know the answer means giving up the fantasy of always moving forward and allowing instead for seasons of dormancy. And it is always time to listen. Perhaps the heart's single greatest desire is to listen attentively to the voice of God speaking through scripture, nature, daily events, and the kind of reflection that leads to expanding self-knowledge....My heart wants the kind of life that leaves room for God."
- What word or phrase stands out to you? Where have your desires edged out room for God? What would it look like for you to leave room for God in what you desire?

---

72 Elizabeth J. Canham, *Heart Whispers: Benedictine Wisdom for Today* (Upper Room, 1999).

day 30: new

"One day you wake up and you realize something, you see
something in a way that you never saw it before, and boom,
epiphany. Something is different forever."

— JOHN GREEN

Songs help me find my feelings and give me words to describe what is happening in my heart and my soul. In a season of spiritual disruption, Sara Groves' songs aided me in naming and understanding. I remember listening to the song "Something Changed" over and over again as I sought to explain the shift I was noticing in my soul. It was as if one day I was content with the status quo and the next I was not. Weirdly, what I felt wasn't restlessness or dissatisfaction but longing. There is more. I want more. God is more.

In my work, I see people in many different stages of spiritual growth and maturity. So far, I have yet to come up with a way to explain how or why people grow, change, and mature. Or why they don't. What I do know is that the deepest changes occur without any help from me—or you. Sure, you can position yourself in ways that make spiritual growth more or less likely. Sure,

205

you can take actions that invite or resist change. But it's like Paul taught the Corinthians, "I planted the seed, Apollos watered the plants, but God made you grow. It's not the one who plants or the one who waters who is at the center of this process but God, who makes things grow." (1 Corinthians 3:7)

God is at the center of the process of your spiritual growth. You see when you are ready to see. You know what you need to know when you need to know it. You mature at just the right time—in just the right way.

You don't have to work so hard to make something new—God is already on it. God's been on it from the start—and you're invited to join God in recreating all things. "Forget about what's happened; don't keep going over old history. Be alert, be present. I'm about to do something brand-new. It's bursting out! Don't you see it?" (Isaiah 43:19) The generative, creative, expansive God is doing a new thing—and you are welcome to witness and participate.

My friend Tiffany Bird is a fellow spiritual director. She gives a picture of how the Examen opened her up to God's recreating work in her life:

> I was taught to pray at a very young age—before meals, at bedtime, and at church gatherings. While I appreciated the rhythm of prayer, I often felt an internal pressure to keep up my prayers so I could please God and earn His favor. The Prayer of Examen opened up a new way for me to trust God's love for me beyond the spiritual activities I maintained. In reflecting on my daily experiences with the Lord, His constant presence in my life became abundantly apparent.

The Examen revealed to me patterns of God's grace woven throughout each of my ordinary days. The most shocking discovery was that these kindnesses—which I would have overlooked without the Examen—weren't tied to my behavior or even my ritual of prayer. They were unearned gifts freely given, whether I took the time to acknowledge them or not. The Lord was clearly working beyond my knowledge for my good as He used my seemingly mundane experiences to uniquely and lovingly draw me to Himself. This simple yet powerful prayer reflection reminds me that God's love constantly reaches out to me, and over time, I have learned to rest in this love rather than continuing to work to try to earn it.

She didn't make it happen or earn the right to have it happen—God gave the growth. And the love, the presence, the faithfulness of God is now hers. And the gift of the Examen is that it can remind you every twenty-four hours that God is at work, that God is doing a new thing. Transformation is less disorienting, less scary when you experience it as gradual and subtle. You might not see the monumental shift taking place—and you might try to stop it if you did—but you can notice the incremental movements toward greater faith, hope and love.

Our family has two goldendoodles—Gracie (the perfect one) and Coco (the neurotic one). We brought Gracie home when she was four months old, and her stated purpose was to be a comfort and companion to our son. She has faithfully served in this role for over thirteen years—served him and the rest of us with abandon.

When I went back through my journals from nine years ago, I was surprised by how stressed out I was about Gracie. I have been accused of being over-responsible, and the evidence was everywhere—I felt overwhelmed by what I perceived as the dog's constant need for attention. I had two young children and a husband who traveled, and at the end of the day I just didn't want to be needed.

Gracie appeared in my Examen at least weekly as a source of frustration and failure. As the kids grew, I stopped seeing Gracie as demanding and even started thinking I could handle another dog. And then I fell for a cute picture my mom texted me of a coworker's dog—a dog the coworker was giving away for free. All I can say is you get what you pay for. That dog is a mess—needier than Gracie ever was. (She's only seven and it feels like a long life with her.)

These days, I take both dogs on a daily walk. Gracie's joy in life is to take the leash in her mouth and prance the last 100 feet home by herself (Coco is completely untrustworthy and has yet to earn such a privilege). I teared up recently as I reviewed my day and thought about Gracie walking with the leash in her mouth. Thirteen is old for a big dog, and her legs are giving out on her daily. But she's faithful and true, and our family will not be the same without her.

I told her recently, "You and I didn't have a great start, but we're gonna end well." Thanks be to God. I did not try to love that dog better. God gave me the growth. My tears over this precious dog today remind me that God indeed changes hearts. (So, God, how about some movement toward loving Coco?)

ALL THE MORE

- Think back to consolation and desolation—how consolation involves feeling drawn and desolation involves feeling driven. As you ponder your day, where did you notice your drivenness to make something happen? Where did you feel drawn to something new God is doing?

- In which areas of your life do you long for growth or maturity? Tell God about it. Ask for eyes to see how God is giving you the growth—even if it's tiny baby steps.

- When you feel discouraged or stuck, make a list of all that God grows, makes, or does without any help from you—sunrises, babies in the womb, flowers, etc. God's nature is to make and remake. Trust in the faithful work of God.

conclusion

Thanks for sticking with me. I consider it an honor to journal these words for you. I'm blown away that you read them. My deepest desire is that you prayed them. That they found their way into your soul and gently guided you to greater faith, hope, and love.

I'm thankful I got to share one of my spiritual heroes, St. Ignatius, with you. I pray that the path he journeyed before us provides sure footing for your own travels with God. I hope it's something. It won't be everything—I know that for sure! But your time spent praying the Examen is not nothing.

Now is when I really wish we were sitting across from other another in my sunroom. You could tell me what words jumped out at you, what stayed with you, what confused, inspired, or bored you. You could tell me what you've started paying attention to—what you see now that you didn't before. I would listen and tell you that I'm so excited. Why excited? Because I've witnessed this one prayer open more doors than the most eager of church greeters ever could. I know that on the other side of the Examen, you will tell me stories.

Who knows how long it might be until we are face to face. But I will be cheering you on and trusting in the God who made you to light your way—all the way home to yourself, to those you love, and to God's own heart. You're going to make it. One twenty-four-hour day at a time. One prayer at a time.

Writing these words and offering them to you has been healing for me. I hope healing is a part of what God does with them in your life. If that's the case, hear these words from Maya Angelou, "As soon as healing takes place, go out and heal somebody else." Offer what you've learned to someone else. It's what you do in consolation, it's what moves you out of desolation. It's how you keep the gifts you've been given.

acknowledgments

Kudos to my friends and family members who did not burst out laughing, grimace, or give me side-eye when I said I was writing a book. Thank you for acting like it was the most natural thing for me to do. Thank you for offering to read it, buy it, and sell it for me at your place of work.

Thank you to the team at Morgan James Publishing for believing in this book and taking a chance on me. Thanks to David Hancock, Jim Howard, Tom Dean, Stephanie McLawhorn, and Karen Anderson for making me an author.

Thanks to Sissi Haner for being a detail-oriented miracle worker. The fact that you are reading a fully formatted and edited book from my original Word document is all her hard work. I'm grateful for her patience with me during this process—and for answering every question with grace.

Thank you to my early readers—Summer Curwen, Susan Swoboda, Max Weiss, Meeka Karger, Sarah Braud, Stacey Perry, Amy Nuzback, Crista Stewart, and Sonja Lowell—for your time, enthusiasm, and feedback. Thank you to Kelsi Ray, Cari Stone, Jennifer Barham, Samantha Jay, Bekah Pogue, and Renee Farkas for going above and beyond in helping me make this a better book.

Thank you to all those who shared their stories with me so that I could share them with my readers. Renee Farkas, Virginia Bousquet, Lynn Lavender, Tiffany Bird, Cari Stone, Nancy Baughman, Julia Halford, Vanessa Sadler, and Heather Flener—I'm so grateful for the time spent with each of you.

Thank you to my spiritual directors over the last ten years—Renee Farkas, Scott Owings, Kathy Koellein, and Sandy Wilson—and to spiritual directors everywhere—for choosing to hold space for the seeking soul. Special thanks to Lucy Malone, a dear spiritual director friend, for the use of her beautiful carriage house. It was there that the idea for the book came to me and there that some of the most significant writing took place.

Thank you to those who undertook the Spiritual Exercises with me that first year. God gave me so many graces through your stories and love. Thank you to all those whom I have had the privilege of being in spiritual direction groups with and those who have been in my spiritual direction groups. I learn so much from each of you.

Thank you to those who write books and those who make sure books get into as many hands as possible. You indulged this first-time writer generously and made me feel like I could do it. Big love to Patsy Clairmont, Karen Anderson, Andi Ashworth, Don Pape, Bekah Pogue, and Steve Garber.

Thank you to The Refuge Center for Counseling and The Public Franklin for allowing me to invest time and energy into things I care about. I'm honored to help bring awareness and wholeness to mental health and racial equity by serving on boards with some of the best people I know.

Thank you to my friends and family. I'm surrounded by love, and I wouldn't make it without my people. I'm so grateful for friends who buoy me and sustain me. I'm grateful for family who provides me with roots and wings—AND makes holidays and family dinners fun. I wouldn't trade any of you.

Thank you to Dan, Noah, Max, Gracie, and Coco—the most frequent guest stars in my daily Examen. No one else has taught me more.

I do not know why or how my eyes were opened to the astounding generosity and humility of Jesus through the Spiritual Exercises. I only know that I will never be the same. Thank you, Jesus, for showing me the huge heart of God and beckoning me gently and lovingly to it every single day.

appendix

I've included a chart if you're curious about your Enneagram type's relationship with the Centers. Notice that three types (3, 6, 9) have a more complicated relationship with the Centers. Their Preferred and Repressed Centers are the same. Threes lead with feelings (others) and have to work to feel their own. Sixes think (i.e., worry) constantly but struggle with productive thinking. Nines Do first, but it looks more like puttering, and Intentional Doing is the challenge for them. For more on the Enneagram and the three Centers of Intelligence, I highly recommend Suzanne and Joe Stabile's Spiritual Practices and the Enneagram workshop and audio course[73] and Adele and Doug Calhoun's book, *Spiritual Rhythms for the Enneagram*. Chart credit to Suzanne Stabile in *Know Your Number*.

The second chart shows your Enneagram type's Core Fears and Desires. As mentioned in chapter three, we are all running toward something. The Enneagram calls this our Core Desire.

Along with running toward something, we are all running away from something. The Enneagram calls this our Core Fear.

---

73 "Spiritual Practices and the Enneagram," Life in the Trinity Ministry, https:// www.lifeinthetrinityministry.com/store/spe.

The 3 Enneagram Centers

Enneagram Type	Preferred Center	Support Center	Repressed Center
One	Doing	Feeling	Thinking
Two	Feeling	Doing	Thinking
Three	Feeling (Unacknowledged feelings)	Thinking / Doing	Feeling (Acknowledged feelings)
Four	Feeling	Thinking	Doing
Five	Thinking	Feeling	Doing
Six	Thinking (Unproductive)	Feeling / Doing	Thinking (Productive)
Seven	Thinking	Doing	Feeling
Eight	Doing	Thinking	Feeling
Nine	Doing (Unintentional)	Thinking / Feeling	Doing (Intentional)

Core Desires and Core Fears by Enneagram Type

Enneagram Type	Core Desire	Core Fear
One	Being good/right	Being bad/wrong
Two	Being loved and wanted	Being unwanted or unworthy of love
Three	Being admired, successful, respected	Being worthless, considered a failure
Four	Being unique, special, authentic	Being inadequate, plain, insignificant
Five	Being capable and competent	Being incapable and incompetent
Six	Having security, guidance, support	Not having security, guidance, support
Seven	Being happy, satisfied, content	Being trapped in pain or boredom
Eight	Being able to protect oneself and others	Being controlled or manipulated
Nine	Having inner stability and peace of mind	Losing connection with self and others

resources

Ignatian Spirituality Resources

Books

Barry, William A., SJ. *Finding God in All Things: A Companion to the Spiritual Exercises of St. Ignatius.* Notre Dame, IN: Ave Maria Press, 1991.

Barry, William A., SJ. *Letting God Come Close: An Approach to the Ignatian Spirituality Exercises.* Chicago: Loyola Press, 2001.

Fleming, David L., SJ. *What is Ignatian Spirituality?* Chicago: Loyola Press, 2008.

Gallagher, Timothy M. *The Discernment of Spirits: An Ignatian Guide for Everyday Living.* New York: Crossroad Publishing, 2005.

Healey, Fr Charles J., SJ. *The Ignatian Way: Key Aspects of Jesuit Spirituality.* New York: Paulist Press, 2009.

Martin, Fr James, SJ. *The Jesuit Guide to (Almost) Everything: A Spirituality for Real Life.* New York: HarperOne, 2012.

Silf, Margaret. *Inner Compass: An Invitation to Ignatian Spirituality.* Chicago: Loyola Press, 1999.

Tetlow, Joseph A. SJ. *Ignatius Loyola: Spiritual Exercises.* New York: Crossroad Publishing, 1992.

Thibodeaux, Mark E. *God's Voice Within: The Ignatian Way to Discover God's Will.* Chicago: Loyola Press, 2010.

Websites

Onlineministries.Creighton.Edu/CollaborativeMinistry: Creighton University's online ministries, including a retreat of the Spiritual Exercises based on the 19th Annotation.

Jesuits.org: The Society of Jesus

Pray-As-You-Go.org: A new prayer session is produced every day of the working week and one session for the weekend.

SacredSpace.ie: Your daily prayer online.

IgnatianSpirituality.com: Provides pathways into the major areas of Ignatian spirituality.

Apps

Pray as You Go: iOS and Android links can be found at the bottom of Pray-As-You-Go.org

Reimagining the Examen: iOS and Android links can be found at the bottom of Reimaginingexamen.IgnatianSpirituality.com

Enneagram Resources

Calhoun, Adele and Doug Calhoun and Clare and Scott Lough-rige. *Spiritual Rhythms for the Enneagram: A Handbook for Harmony and Transformation*. Westmont, IL: IVP, 2019.

Cron, Ian Morgan and Suzanne Stabile. *The Road Back to You: An Enneagram Journey of Self-Discovery*. Westmont, IL: IVP, 2016.

McCord, Beth and Jeff McCord. *Becoming Us: Using the Enneagram to Create a Thriving Gospel-Centered Marriage*. New York: Morgan James, 2019.

Riso, Don Richard and Russ Hudson. *The Wisdom of the Enneagram: The Complete Guide to Psychological and Spiritual Growth for the Nine Personality Types*. New York: Bantam, 1999.

Riso, Don Richard and Russ Hudson. *Understanding the Enneagram: The Practical Guide to Personality Types*. Boston: Mariner Books, 2000.

Rohr, Richard and Andreas Ebert. *The Enneagram: A Christian Perspective*. New York: Crossroad Publishing, 2001.

Stabile, Suzanne. *The Path Between Us: An Enneagram Journey to Healthy Relationships*. Westmont, IL: IVP, 2018.

Vancil, Marilyn. Self to Lose, Self to Find: A Biblical Approach to the 9 Enneagram Types. Enumclaw, WA: Redemption Press, 2016.

Wagele, Elizabeth. *The Enneagram of Parenting: The 9 Types of Children and How to Raise Them Successfully*. New York: HarperOne, 1997.

about the author

Katie Haseltine is a trained Spiritual Director, a certified Enneagram coach, and a self-care coach. After trying too hard for most of her life, Katie found rest in the words of Jesus—love God with all your heart, mind, and body and love others as you love yourself. The ancient practices of spiritual direction, the Enneagram, and the Examen ushered Katie into a fuller, richer relationship with God, herself, and others—and compelled her to offer another way to others like her. Katie lives with her family in Franklin, Tennessee.

A free ebook edition is available with the purchase of this book.

To claim your free ebook edition:

1. Visit MorganJamesBOGO.com
2. Sign your name CLEARLY in the space
3. Complete the form and submit a photo of the entire copyright page
4. You or your friend can download the ebook to your preferred device

Print & Digital Together Forever.

Snap a photo

Free ebook

Read anywhere